CW00542862

Raising Awareness, Ending Exploitation

Edited by Carrie Pemberton, Alison Myers
and Lucy Berry

British Library Cataloguing in Publication data
A catalogue record for this book is available from the British library.

ISBN 978-1-9095958-11-5

First published by Inspire
4 John Wesley Road
Werrington
Peterborough
PE4 6ZP

Printed and bound in Great Britain by Aldridge Print Group, Mitcham, Surrey

Contents

Love Is

Love is patient and kind.
It deceives no one. It kidnaps no one. It rapes no one.

Love is never selfish.
It does not lust for money, power, or prostitutes.

Love always hopes.
It protects, encourages and transforms.

Love will never come to an end.

Inspired by 1 Corinthians 13

Foreword

I welcome this important book. Its combination of factual pieces, reflections, poetry and true stories will improve understanding of human trafficking and encourage more people to get involved in putting a stop to it.

Before becoming an MP I worked with young people who had been sexually abused. The combination of that dreadful wrong with the transportation of people across frontiers is sickening. One of the important parts of my job as Minister for Women and Equality between 2005-07 was to raise awareness of the nature of this crime and to strengthen our support systems for its victims

There are a large number of different ways women are trafficked into the UK for sexual exploitation, such as:

- fictitious advertisements in the country of origin
- fictitious advertisements for marriages
- kidnapping, often in regions devastated by war, where economic and social infrastructures have collapsed
- girls sold by their families
- grooming of adolescent girls by so called 'boyfriends' who are part of the criminal trafficking network, and
- women locked into paying off serial debt bondage.

Once in the hands of their 'minders', women face an appalling future. These exploited young women are kept in conditions akin to slavery. Here in the UK we do have tough sentences for traffickers and the law is rigorously enforced against those who commit sexual crimes against women involved in prostitution; but if the demand did not exist, the numbers involved in trafficking would be greatly reduced.

This book asks the important question of why we continue to regard the buying and selling of sex as acceptable. Wherever there are prostitutes, there will be trafficked women. We shouldn't accept that prostitution is the 'oldest profession' and that, therefore, it will always be with us!

No young girl starts out in life thinking that she would like to be a prostitute when she grows up. Women end up in prostitution through many routes. We can do more to tackle the reasons that women become prostitutes, but we also have to focus on the men who exploit women.

Changing attitudes is never easy but campaigns do work. We can look back 200 years to the campaign that led to the abolition of the slave trade, or to the Jubilee 2000 campaign that put pressure on governments to take debt relief seriously for the poorest nations of the earth.

Our Christian beliefs must surely mean that we have to assert everyone's humanity? How can it be right for anyone to buy sex? Isn't it time we made it illegal?

I want to congratulate CHASTE, the Churches Alert to Sex Trafficking across Europe, and the Revd Dr Carrie Pemberton, who have been working to raise awareness of the trafficking of women for sexual exploitation. This book is a valuable addition to this work.

Meg Munn, *Member of Parliament for Sheffield Heeley, Minister for Women and Equality, May 2005 – June 2007*

Introduction:

The ABC of Trafficking for Sexual Exploitation

How it Works

A. The cycle of demand. The trafficking business is now worth an estimated £10.5 billion globally. Traffickers are part of an international network supplying demand for sex as a commodity; the women and children whom they entrap are their food chain. The cycle is infused with deception and brutality.

B. The sting. A young woman or minor is offered new opportunities and financial rewards in Japan, Europe, or North America. This might be waitressing or secretarial opportunities, cultural events, or light-end sexual entertainment work. One 15-year-old in Lithuania was told she'd be earning money for her next year's academic fees through selling ice cream in the UK.

C. The story behind the sting is that women may already be vulnerable to entrapment. You'll see that many times in testimonies in this book. Women caught in sex-trafficking often come from backgrounds where there is domestic abuse and violence against women.

D. This isn't everybody's story. Many trafficked women are seeking improvement and opportunities outside of their own countries – and are bitterly deceived.

E. For women who have some history already in prostitution (and there are some), they have no idea of what awaits them in their country of enslavement. Their passport and visa papers are taken away the moment they are through immigration control.

F. Women are frequently told they are now the 'property' of the person whom they now live with. They will be intimidated, beaten and raped by their de facto pimp.

G. They are given a bill for the cost of their travel, location and management.

H. The sum increases all the time, with 'fines' added for failure to 'perform'.

I. Clothing and food allowances are added. This is the modern form of debt-bondage. One young Nigerian woman, whom CHASTE has worked with, had a vast 'debt' accrued. She had worked a 70-hour-week for 3 years and 'owed' more than £30,000.

J. Unlike the lithographs of African-slave markets, modern slave 'sales' take place in bars, basements, airport lounges and streets across Europe.

K. Women and young girls change hands for as little as £500, rising to £20,000 for an exceptionally beautiful, virginal specimen.

L. These prisoners rarely manage to escape. They are too frightened and traumatized to try to leave. They are beaten up. Broken bones are not uncommon.

M. They are raped and verbally abused. They are psychologically manipulated: slave-owners often promise to hurt their family back home, or to humiliate them publicly to their former peers or former work colleagues.

N. Simply having a pistol placed in their mouth usually secures control. The cynical violence knows no bounds.

O. How do clients know if a woman is a slave? Knowing that she is foreign isn't a clue; 70 per cent of workers in our massage parlours and brothels are now in this category.

P. She might be reluctant to 'work'. She may have cigarette burns, knife marks or razor cuts from self-harming.

Q. Deputy Chief Constable Grahame Maxwell, the director of the United Kingdom Human Trafficking Centre, has said that anyone who pays for sex with a woman who is then found to have been trafficked will be charged with rape. What a clear signal to the purchasing market: don't collude in trafficking.

R. Very rarely, strangers, taxi drivers, concerned women in nightclubs, or extremely alert church, health or social-workers help women to escape.

S. More frequently women are 'surfaced' or 'rescued' by police counter-vice operations or immigration raids. When a woman hasn't got the right papers she is invited to an interview at a police reception centre or station.

T. If she is from one of the ten most trafficked countries, she's given immediate reassurance and information in her mother tongue courtesy of a CHASTE initiative using iPod technology. She is provided with a Home Office approved interpreter as soon as possible. She is debriefed as quickly as possible on her situation and wishes.

U. This debriefing process is much better than it was. The newly formed United Kingdom Human Trafficking Centre has meant that new financial resources are flowing in to train frontline personnel in the immigration, police, social services and medical services, so they can quickly identify women who have been trafficked.

V. An identified woman is offered a place in a government-sponsored house or a house provided by a faith community. Until September 2006, there were only 27 designated safe beds in the UK, paid for by the Home Office. In 2007 this rose to 47, due to the CHASTE Safe Housing initiative, which has brought the energies and commitment of the Medaille Trust and the Salvation Army into housing provision.

W. Four thousand women are being trafficked into the UK for sexual exploitation every year.

X. Some women have found a safe haven, a future and a hope in the UK. Others have gone back to their own country; their situations are less certain. One thing is for sure ...

Y. Helping individual women and children isn't enough. Alterations in the law and more resources are essential if trafficking is to be halted. Until the UK addresses the demand for pay-as-you-go sex, women will continue to be tricked and betrayed. The UK is morally accountable. Money, personal involvement, local-church involvement and denominational involvement are needed now.

Z. We are praying that this anthology helps you understand the terrible evil which is going on in Britain now. We need you. How will you get involved?

Testimony and Witness

If you have ears, then hear.

Jesus

The beginning of CHASTE: Portia's story

CHASTE was born, as a tiny fledgling, on the day I first met Portia and her three children. I was the Religious Manager at Yarls Wood Immigration Centre, and had been called by the duty Detention Custody Officer in C Wing to see whether I could help. I had just finished the Sunday Eucharist and was preparing to return home to lunch with my family. I was told that a mother, recently arrived in the Family Unit, was 'incoherent, suicidal and hysterical'; what was the cause? I quickly rang my husband to explain that I would be somewhat delayed, and asked him to apologize to our children that our family roast would be partaken without my presence.

Portia's children were being looked after in the Yarls Wood crèche and school facility when we first met. She spoke fluent Portuguese but only a smattering of English. I spoke English and not a syllable of Portuguese. There was no one in the centre who knew Portuguese or Spanish. So, we were at the mercy of Language-Line, a phone-based language facility, which is widely used by UK prisons, health services, police and social services to resolve such day-to-day breakdowns in communications. But Language-Line comes at a price, and the phone call which Portia and I had took place in the hearing of Detention Custody Officers.

As soon as I grasped the level of Portia's terror, and the reasons for it, I took her back to her bedroom. There, with a Portuguese Bible, an English Bible and a few words of commonly shared French, we began to build up some trust and take some faltering steps towards safety.

Psalm 23 was our starting point. 'The Lord is my Shepherd, so shall I lack nothing', declares the first stanza of this ancient Middle Eastern text.

'Celui-ci,' insisted Portia, 'celui-ci j'en ai besoin.' 'This, this is what I need.' I looked around the bare walls of the twin-bedded room where we were sitting; ubiquitous institutional lemon, a single shelf above the bed. Portia sat holding my hand, shuddering occasionally, weeping intermittently.

Portia's home life had been ripped apart by a combination of political upheaval, commercial greed, criminality and malice across two continents and three nations: Africa and Europe, Angola, Portugal and the UK.

She had initially fled from a violent attack on her family, who were part of an extended clan which contested political leadership in Central Africa. Her flight to Europe had been facilitated by a smuggling ring who brought her to Portugal. However, once she was there they demanded extra payment which embroiled Portia in prostitution in a Lisbon brothel.

When she'd worked there for over three years, the traffickers started to turn their attentions on her eldest child, then a pubescent girl of twelve years old. This triggered the required energy Portia needed to escape from Lisbon and travel to the United Kingdom. As one of our psychotherapists explained to our safe-house personnel, you don't just flee from disaster, you need to be able to flee towards safety. In Liverpool she hid from the authorities, for two years, until one day in early summer she was picked up from her flat by the immigration authorities. They had raided her place of work, and found that she had inappropriate papers.

Portia was from a Catholic background, but had been supported by Jehovah's Witnesses while staying and working in her flat. She had a range of needs which required immediate attention.

First, her trafficking background hadn't been properly understood by the immigration authorities in charge of her case. Her legal counsel had been inadequate and her plea needed to be altered. She had failed to submit a thorough account of her history or an appeal for asylum. But, if she was released now from the detention centre she would have no place of safety and no recourse to public funding. She would be destitute.

Second, from a medical point of view, it wasn't clear how healthy she was. The usual health risks of sex-trafficked women are clearly spelt out in a report undertaken for the European Union 2003. These include the effects of vaginal, oral or anal sex, unwanted pregnancies, forced abortion and the misuse of oral contraceptives.

The medical outcomes of sex-slavery include physical fatigue, poor nutrition, nerve, muscle or bone damage, dental problems, lacerations, head trauma, damage to the vaginal tract, irritable bowel syndrome, stress-related syndromes, urinary tract infections, cystitis, cervical cancer and infertility. Most trafficked women who have been prostituted, carry on average twelve major health impacts in their bodies and psyches from the traumas of their sexual abuse and rigours of kidnap, intimidation and isolation from their support networks.

Third, there were questions to be asked about the mental and emotional damage which Portia might have sustained as a result of such psychological abuse. On top of this, of course she was living right on the margins with no economic support.

Finally (and only very few studies even comment on this aspect of trauma), there were Portia's spiritual needs. We prayed Psalm 23 together, as Portia's trauma and terror poured out in a stream of tears and emotion which shook her whole body. She was so like a frail animal, cornered, awaiting the final bullet of the hunter.

There wasn't much time to intervene on Portia's behalf. But getting out the key elements of her story, her unbelievably brutal experiences, was the essential start to moving her to a place of safety. By the end of the afternoon I had enough information to be able to contact an expert human rights lawyer who could come to Portia's – and her children's – aid.

I left Portia that evening knowing that, although still on suicide watch, she would be with us the following morning when I came back into work. She had visibly calmed, and promised not to damage the life which God had given her – even though she still felt 'in the valley of death'.

Once David, Portia's newly acquired lawyer, had swung into action to stay her removal order, we had less than 24 hours to arrange alternative accommodation for her and her children. Thankfully her friends from the Jehovah's Witnesses came good. They could offer her immediate accommodation in the city from which she had come. On Tuesday evening, less than 72 hours after first meeting Portia, she was collected with her children and taken away to safety back in Liverpool.

As I waved her goodbye, I was overcome with a sense of relief and gratitude. Relief that the transport taking her away was a family car, with friends whom she had already met, and not the Group 4 transit van which transports 'detainees' to Heathrow for removal. Gratitude that I had participated in a journey, which although still in process, was moving towards greener pastures and away from evil.

My cup ran over! I stood there in full view of the custody officers – and cried.

There were other 'Portias' whom I met during my time at Yarls Wood before it burnt down during a riot on the evening of Valentine's Day 2002. Some of them I was able to assist in the same way as Portia. Others desperately, unfairly, pathetically, were extracted from this last tentative toe-hold of safety and sent back to their country of origin.

Portia was the first woman to have told me face to face in stuttering, terrified sound bites her story of trafficking abuse. A staff had been put into my hand which I couldn't put down.

When I moved on from Yarls Wood after the fire, I remembered Portia and all the other trafficked women from other countries. I wondered how to move things on so that there would always be places of safety for them to turn to, whether they had children or not.

I believed (and still do), as a minister, that churches and faith communities have an invaluable part to play as good Samaritans. It was clear to me that this is Jesus' mandate to the churches today; to provide safety, shelter and space for recovery for those set upon by thieves. The concept of CHASTE had been born.

On a chilly morning in October 2004, two-and-a-half years after meeting Portia, I received a significant letter and an extraordinary phone call. The letter was from the Charity Commissioners telling me that CHASTE had been accepted as a registered charity to undertake work on behalf of those surviving trafficking for sexual exploitation. I was jubilant!

Later in the week, as I'd just waved my children off to school, the phone rang and I answered it thinking it was one of the kids who'd forgotten something.

'What is it?' I asked.

'Hello,' answered a wonderful hybrid accent of Portuguese-African-settling-into-English-voice (somewhat surprised at my tone). 'It's Portia.'

'Portia!' I squeaked. 'Hello! How are you? Where are you? Is everything Ok with you?'

'Yes, Pastor,' she said, 'it's OK. I'm here in my flat. How are you, Pastor? How are your children? How is your husband? I hope they are all well. I have wonderful news – and want to thank you so much for what you did. I have been granted refugee status here in the UK! Isn't that great? It's so wonderful! And the children are so well and happy. God has been so kind!'

My head (and the initial work of CHASTE) was truly anointed with oil.

© Carrie Pemberton, Chief Executive Officer, CHASTE
Portia is not this woman's real name. It means 'blessed'.

From cruel to vicious

They have to stand for hours a day while men come to look them over.
They look at their breasts, the colour of their skin and check to see if they have rashes or pimples. The girls have to dress up to look like prostitutes and put on make-up. Those who resist are isolated, beaten and terrorized. It's even more humiliating for them if they are considered ugly. They are treated worse than animals in what they are forced to do. You have a full range of traffickers from cruel to vicious.

© V. Malarek, The Natashas *(Victory Press 2002)*

African trafficking: it cannot stand

Trafficking in human lives is generally defined as the slave trade of the twenty-first century. It is often implied that the slave trade, in all forms and expressions, has long been abolished. This is not the case. Rather than a *re*-occurrence, the sad picture is that of permanence and perpetuation of the phenomenon.

In other words, slavery never ended, was never abolished, but has remained as a *modus operandi*, an integral part of society, civilization, progress and tradition.

This is particularly pertinent to some African cultures and traditions, whose regimes have fuelled and instigated the subjection and exploitation of women. They have also contributed heavily to the supply chain in the international market of sex slavery.

The mere idea of the birth of a female child is already the beginning of enslavement in these cultures. Male children are preferred and wished for. Most families find it natural to 'sacrifice' the education of girls, as it is believed that their roles in the society never go any further than wives and mothers.

By virtue of their exclusion from 'un-necessary' education, these women are to be eternally cared for and protected by men who are capable of possessing them as properties or 'personal items', bought and paid for, as it were.

By way of contradiction, these same women are daily faced with the challenges of proving the worth of their womanhood through heroic acts that range from raising a family single-handedly to becoming the breadwinner of the family. They are once again called to be offered as 'sacrificial lambs' for the economic salvation of their entire lineage, irrespective of age and feasible capability.

The young African women trafficked to and across Europe cannot be said to have made a conscious decision to get involved. Often, such decisions are made behind their backs and they do not understand what they are getting into. It is this lack of negotiation – or any clear picture of what Europe would look like – that makes the job of recruiters and traffickers so easy, and makes the victims their easy prey.

Poverty is the main cause or 'push factor' of trafficking. This is not exclusively the case. But impoverishment has no one single definition. Like riches, poverty comes in many forms. The Bible shows us that time and again.

Another major, profound root cause is globalization, particularly the absurd, pacific, co-existence of poverty and opulence. In other words, it is not a question simply of being poor without options; it is a question of living in poverty, in the same vicinity as a next-door neighbour who constantly parades his suddenly acquired wealth. It is important to recognize that what is often referred to as 'wealth' is nothing other than a better condition of living, a family house and a second-hand car. It is appalling that families are willing to sacrifice their daughters in the same way that Esau was ready to exchange his birthright for a pot of porridge.

Religion and religious beliefs constitute an essential element in the trafficking of African women. In the first place, some new churches have implemented selective reading of the Bible which encourages false hopes. It convinces believers that material wealth goes hand in hand with faith and is a right, owed to them by God, which they are entitled to claim. These churches, in simple terms, preach that an end justifies its means; dispensing with conscience and the sense of sin.

There are instances where church leaders misuse their positions. The much feared 'voodoo rite', undergone by most trafficked Nigerian women, provokes so much terror in them that it prevents them from breaking free from their situation of bondage. This sometimes carries religious overtones. It is a violation of what they hold most sacred; an act of violence to their right to belief and faith in the Almighty.

Addressing the issue of gender equality in African countries constitutes a vital milestone in the global fight against trafficking. Given the huge role played by African women in the entire process and procedure of trafficking, the situation could be rightly defined as a kingdom divided against itself.

It cannot stand.

Bad choices, plus injustice: Albania

This is no place for her life.
The sum of her youth
Can't lead her to be a housewife;
High dreams but low means.

A cell keeps her dreams caged;
Bad choices plus injustice.
She cries out from dead eyes
Living to break free.

Her life can't get any worse.
All hope
Is false hope.
She just can't break free.

A deceiver she trusts in
Adds insult to injury.
She leaves home believing.
At the end,
No boyfriend.
She didn't break free.

In some dark alley brothel
They take away her freedom.
What they sell is her dignity.
She can't cope,
Without hope,
Desperate to break free.

But now I am pregnant

My boy friend, well, he brought me to Italy, with two friends of his. He said it would be better for us in Italy. The night after we arrived, he drove me to this area on the outskirts of the city (Naples) and told me to start working. There was nothing I could do. He and his two friends were watching me, making sure I did my work. After a year they said we were going to the UK, as they could make more money there. I didn't want to have sex with all the men who came. There were sometimes twenty or more a day. But I was beaten if I didn't work. In the end, you just don't care ...

But now I am pregnant and I want to look after her or him.

He/she is the only person I have in the world to love.

From Nigeria – through Ghana – to Holland – 2005

There were about a dozen other women who were brought out of Ghana with me. I didn't see them again but I met others where I worked. I worked six hours on the street, and seven hours in a sex parlour. I was so exhausted I only went home to sleep. Every week someone came to fetch the money I made on the streets. When I started to sleep, instead of work I was beaten up. I still owe at least £20,000 in debt to those who trafficked me – I can't see how I shall ever be free.

I am Amoti

I am Amoti. This was one of the most significant days of my life. My little ramshackle stall, made of woven matete, was weighed down with plastic bags filled with tap water to sell to the thirsty commuters of Lagos. A flamboyantly dressed Yoruba woman approached me. 'Would you like to come and look after my children rather than sell water on the streets?' she asked me. Within hours my life had been transformed. At Mama Edi's house I looked after two small boisterous children, while Mama undertook her import–export business. I had my own room! And my clothes provided for me. Not since before my parents died from HIV/AIDS had I been so happy. Time passed, the children were ready to go to secondary school and my work changed to that of assistant housekeeper in Mama Edi's Lagos compound.

One day, after a particularly long and enthusiastic church service, Mama Edi introduced me to a friend of hers who lived in Great Britain! She was so friendly and excited to offer me the post of a nanny to her young son – in a house overlooking the River Thames! In no time I was on a plane to London, with smart, warm clothes for the cold British weather. But the plane landed in Dublin, and Mama Edi's friend did not meet me. Another woman, Mama Luka, who was Ghanaian, met me and brought me to a house. There, instead of a young boy of three, I was met by Winston, a young Ibo man, and three young women about my age. Winston was very friendly, took me by the hand and showed me to my room. After a cup of tea together and some bread and Blue-Band, he raped me. This was my work from now on. To be ready to receive and entertain the men whom Mama Luka arranged to come to the house. Did I understand? Did I know how to use Durex?

I cried, I pleaded no, this is not what I wanted, not what I had come for, where were the children? I wanted to look after Mama Edi's friend's son – but Winston did not listen. I was left sobbing on the bed – my new blouse bought only two days ago in the market in Lagos was ripped. My thoughts were confused. My hope for a new life was shattered.

Amoti's story is the combination of three young Nigerian women's accounts. These and several other young African women have been helped by CHASTE to access safe housing and support whilst their cases are heard by Asylum tribunals. The majority of these young women are currently returned to their source countries under current UK immigration law and lacunae in counter-trafficking legislation and protection.

What might the Bible offer to those made victims by sex-trafficking?

Let us say this right at the beginning ... Your story isn't here.

There are many stories here; many stories. And some of them are as dense with pain and desperation, with exploitation and deception, as anything that might have happened in your story. There are stories here where the System, despite the usual grand pronouncements about justice and decency, remains as disinterested and cynical, as relentlessly deaf to those who suffer, as anything you may have experienced. There are stories here as layered in awfulness and anger as anything you have lived. So even though your story is not here, there could be things here for you – echoes, parallels, connections, emotions – things that might begin to help.

For a start, some of these stories make it clear that even the ugliest of stories can be told.

No matter what brutality and threats and shame and silence and rage others may have forced into your story ... no matter how much of who you are has been stolen or trampled or ground down, these stories tell you this ... somewhere, when the time is right, **YOUR STORY CAN BE TOLD.**

Another thing. Through these stories, God challenges anyone who wants to be part of the people of God to seek out the sufferer and bind the wounds of those who hurt; listen honestly to the voices of those who have been silenced, share in making community with those who have been pushed to the margins, or beyond.

Now, it's no secret that the story of the Church is too full of stories of failure, of self-serving, sucking up to the System and exploitation of the weak, but God has never given up.

In every generation, these stories continue to challenge people to build communities of resistance, to keep alive even the most dangerous memories, make places for the safe telling of silenced stories, share in a common humanity with the storytellers.

So sometime, somewhere, you may meet people who will acknowledge your hurt, stay with you as you seek to recover who you might be and what you have lost. You may meet people prepared to march alongside you when the failure of the system has to be named, shamed and changed. Whatever they call themselves, wherever you find them, these people who care are responding to the challenge of these stories, these people are living as the people of God.

Your story may not be here, but these stories are out there for you, **CHALLENGING PEOPLE TO BE YOUR FRIENDS**, no matter how desperate your situation, how compromised you may feel, how hard it is to live with yourself, how crushed, dehumanized or silenced you believe yourself to be.

There may be a third thing here for you – the strange stories of God told in these texts. In Old Testament and in New, stories tell of God longing for justice. Other stories tell of the way that God sees everything, even the uglinesses that the System ignores and the betrayals that the world seeks to cover over.

But more than this, God's story tells how Jesus, as God-in-person, has deliberately *entered* our story, risking all the deceit and exploitation, the shame and degradation that our world can fling at him. In these stories, God experiences for himself what it is like to be left betrayed and alone, exploited and denied.

In these stories God experiences the elegant apologies the System makes, even as it washes its hands of you and allows those who would crush, exploit and destroy you to take you and do their worst. Whatever your story tells of degradation and dehumanization, God has been there before you.

Yet God's story of defeat contains a seed of hope. The Gospels do not tell us directly of Jesus' resurrection – they simply accept it has happened. Rather, the Gospels choose to tell stories of the resurrection of trapped, failed, hurting people – a coming back to life by would-be followers of Jesus that *his* resurrection has made possible.

The Gospels tell of the resurrection of desperate, broken people like Mary Magdalene and Peter and John and Thomas and that shattered couple on the road to Emmaus. These stories tell of the resurrection of confused, frightened, people who blame themselves for not escaping, or challenging, the forces of deceit and destruction.
So, at its heart, the story of God carries the promise that, whoever you are, whatever has happened, YOU CAN BE BROUGHT BACK TO LIFE.

There are no easy answers here for you, or for God, but there may be something of hope.

Helena

I do not see
What I want not to see;
So I never saw you.

Blank in your cotton clothes,
Cold in your summer things
You must have shivered in my bus one day

Or stopped beside me at a shop window
Desiring the same top for our six-week baby;
Or joined each other on a park bench, maybe,
Black leaves gusting between us.

Now the spring wind whips a stench
In from the river, the fluorescents down below.

Do they dust for prints on soaking stones
And puzzled bits of broken glass?

I saw your picture in the paper,
And now I know you, at last.

© Jeremy Vine

Rape baby

Snatching, not asking,
I used her as rubbish,
Never conceiving
She'd change it around;

Grafting my spite
Onto something so loving,
Seeding my war-zone
As her holy ground,

Fusing my loathing,
My rough un-belonging,
My sex without context,
My push and my shove

Into swelled loveliness,
Beauty from ugliness,
Fullness from emptiness,
Hate, become love.

© Lucy Berry

A box of matches

Better by far to light a candle than curse the darkness.

I didn't experience the slavery of the sex trade, or beatings or imprisonment by pimps. I wasn't forced to leave home with no way back. But I did experience sexual abuse as a child (by my brother) and rape/exploitation as an adult, by a priest.

As I ponder what helped, it wasn't medication, psychiatrists, hospital or leaflets. It was the care and love of others. I was in darkness. Not a darkness of 'sickness' or even 'evil' (though evil was present), but darkness of 'lack of hope'. I was spirit-less. I felt hopeless despair and a longing for my emotional pain and hurt to be soothed somehow.

I took prescription drugs and drink – and I overdosed. Not to kill myself, I never wanted to die, just wanted 'blotto' for a while. This was interpreted as mental illness.

But I wasn't ill. I was without love. Medication only covered the cracks of my despair but didn't heal it. When you're on medication it's hard to ponder your position. I needed to think, to work out what needed to be done. Paradoxically, I didn't want to think, but I desperately needed to.

The thinking I finally did was a horrendous journey. But it took me from self-blame to a position where I could attribute responsibility not to myself, but to the perpetrators. This was very difficult. Grooming, targeting, pressure and manipulation had placed me where everything was my fault.

Years were lost before I could even begin the process towards hope. But, gradually, thanks to a series of friends, colleagues and counsellors, I began that talking and thinking process which kept me on the straight and narrow – and saved my life.

Later it was other survivors of child-abuse who supported me, as we gathered to share our stories, to lessen our isolation and to learn that it wasn't our fault. Throughout everything I had the love of my twin sister, Ann.

Each of those people had matches in their pocket. They lit the candles that lit up my darkness. They actively reached out. They loved without abuse, without strings attached. As I grew older it wasn't just love they gave, but direction.

I began to believe I was capable. The realization that I mattered to people was startling. I blossomed as the candle-light grew. The more I helped others, the more confidence and self-esteem grew. What lessons can be learned? The darkness can be very dark. But loving people can walk alongside and not give up.

Of course I couldn't leave one significant Person out – Jesus. He has been a faithful, loving companion for so long. He probably knew what my mission in life was going to be.

I have become a leading specialist on Christianity and abuse, and disability and abuse.

I have a purpose in life that is good. And it was people, people, people who got me through – and of course Jesus!

Helping people who have been hurt is never easy. But God says there's no alternative. Carry matches at all times. You may need to light candles.

Josephine Butler – practical mystic

Josephine Butler (1828–1906) is known today for her work with prostitutes. She nursed sick and dying women in her own home. She fought against the injustices caused by the Contagious Diseases Acts of the 1860s, which involved the forcible examination of any women considered likely to have venereal disease. She sought to end trafficking in women.

She was a Christian with a mystical vision which undergirded all her practical activities. As an adolescent, growing up in a home much involved in the abolition of slavery, she struggled with the knowledge of the evil things which humans can do to each other. She wrote:

> Sin seemed to be the law of the world and Satan its master. I could not love God, the God who appeared to my darkened and foolish heart to consent to so much which seemed to me cruel and unjust [...] I asked of the Lord one thing, that he would reveal to me his one, His constant attitude towards his lost world; that as I had showed Him my heart, he would show me his heart [...]
>
> Continuing to make this request through day and night, through summer and winter; with patience and constance, the God who answers prayer had mercy on me; he did not deny me my request of his own heart's love for the sinner and when he makes this revelation, he does more; he makes the enquiring soul a partaker of his own heart's love for the world.
>
> *(Recollections of George Butler (1892), pp. 155–7)*

It was out of this sense of *participation* in God's own love for his creation that Butler's concern for the lost and the outcast originated. It was her way of dealing with the intractable nature of suffering. So when suffering came to her – when her little daughter Eva fell from an upstairs landing to die at her feet – Butler went out to share that too with other sufferers.

It took her to the Workhouse, where she tried to pick oakum with the destitute and prostituted women. A young girl there spoke of the gospel hope to *her* and enabled her to kneel down with them and cry to Jesus in a united, inchoate wail of desire, pain and longing which Butler believed went straight to the heart of God.

So, for Butler, prostituted and trafficked women are never *objects* – even objects of compassionate regard. They are sisters, and we, like them, are in need, if in very different ways, of God's liberation. In her *Autobiographical Memoir* (1909), Butler uses the language of revolutionary socialism to express this sisterhood:

> Womanhood is solidaire. We cannot successfully elevate the standard of public opinion in the matter of justice to woman, and of equality of all in its truest sense, if we are content that a practical, hideous, calculated, manufactured and legally maintained degradation of a portion of womanhood is allowed to go on, before the eyes of all. 'Remember them that are in bonds, as being bound with them.'
>
> Even if we lack the sympathy which makes us feel the chains which bind our enslaved sister, we cannot escape the fact that we are one womanhood; we cannot be wholly and truly free. (p. 285)

Butler shares Paul's sense of the connectedness of humanity which the Church represents and embodies. She quotes the letter to the Hebrews (13.3), about being in bonds with those in bondage. It continues, 'as being yourselves also in the body.' We are all diminished by the treatment of some women and men as mere packages in transit, or as objects for others to own.

Butler believes that just as we should oppose our revulsion towards enslavement with a good sense of connectedness in Christ, so the prostituted woman herself can be both a sign of judgement on the society that allows her enslavement (Butler uses abolitionist terms to describe prostitution as slavery), and also a figure of hope. Her need for liberation is a prophetic sign of creation groaning in the birth-pangs of the need for God's Kingdom:

> The groaning and travailing earth shall be released from her bondage, and the rod of the oppressor shall be broken! Fetters shall no longer be wrought out of the intelligence and civilisation of one zone to entrap the unwary simplicity and enslave the generations of another. The light of day will fall upon all the dark places of the earth, now full of the habitations of cruelty, and there shall come forth, at the call of the Deliverer, the thousands and tens of thousands of the daughters of men now enslaved in all lands to cruelty and lust.
>
> *(The Hour Before the Dawn (1871), p. 110)*

Humanist discourse attacks objectification because it does not treat people as ends in themselves; but Christianity attacks it in a different way, believing that we are not ends in ourselves, but signs and images of the Divine. So there is bad objectification that denies our full humanity and created-ness, and a 'good' version in which we are the radiant sons and daughters of God.

It was Josephine Butler's gift to share the heart of God's love for the world and see in the outcast women of her day not only sisters, but images of the Divine, and the prophets of the liberation of us all.

I am very scared

I said I didn't want to pole-dance any more. I didn't like what I was doing. He then beat me up and raped me. I was sold to this guy who brought me to England – I was to work for him now. If I go back home I won't have a head or legs or hands, they will find me – I am very scared.

Nina

The holy of holies
Has been born on earth again
In this raped place, behind this veil of tears
This scorned, this bleak and abused place

So sad
So desperately sad

The arms that should have enfolded you in tenderness
Came as a sick closet of creeping abuse.

The lips that should have whispered love
Unsheathed teeth of hate, of slash and burn
And from them a biting torrent of shameful ardour spewed.

The ring that wed you
Left a pointing finger,
Led and beat you to a barren field
And exposed you to a vile and naked rain.

All your hopes fell to ruin
Like an untended wall that the wild beasts run over.

Yet a hush has brought you peace
And a shepherd has your healing
In his songs
Of love.

Police detective, South Yorkshire

One of the first cases of trafficking prosecuted under the new counter-trafficking legislation was of a young Lithuanian girl who was told that she would be selling ice creams in the UK. She was only 15 years old and had received a cold-call for a summer vacation job opportunity at her home. After three months of beatings, enforced sex and humiliation, she finally managed to escape her new 'owner'. She had been sold three times in the UK (the last selling-price was a fraction of her original purchase price of £4,000 'as a virgin' when she first arrived at Heathrow). We eventually captured her traffickers through her fantastically brave co-operation.

© CHASTE

Vietnamese testimony

I was in Russia for a while. I went there in order to find safety, but I found myself working for a Russian Madame. I was with another Vietnamese girl, there were many young women working as prostitutes in this quarter of Moscow. I was helped to escape by a Chinese client, who paid for me to come to the United Kingdom. I was raped many times on the journey. When I arrived in the UK on the back of a lorry I managed to escape with my friend. Now I don't know what I am going to do. There is this woman who met me in the local supermarket. She is from my home town, and her husband who runs a restaurant says he will be able to help me. But I don't know them. I think it will be all right. I have nowhere else to stay anyway.

© CHASTE

Abuse of Power

Violence can only be concealed by a lie, and the lie can only be maintained by violence.

Aleksandr Solzhenitsyn

My daughter is nineteen

My daughter is 19. She became a prostitute at the age of 16. Her pimp was her first boyfriend, whom she met when she was 14. He introduced her to crack-cocaine and heroin. She supports both these habits by committing various crimes, including shoplifting, mugging, prostitution, and most recently cheque book/credit card fraud.

Back in September 2002 she was put on a Community Rehabilitation order. Big word, but what does it mean? As long as she turns up weekly for probation she's complying with the conditions of the order. None of the agencies liaise with each other, so really it is just a waste of time.

Social services became involved when she had a baby by her boyfriend at 16. The baby was taken into care and subsequently adopted. I thought at least I would receive some sort of help – but no one listened to what I was saying. As her mum, I had no rights whatsoever. My daughter was – and still is – totally out of control, with no agency willing to take any action which might help stop her. On occasions they have actively supported her to refuse my help.

She has had two thrombosis blood clots in her right leg, open weeping ulcers on her leg, and last August was diagnosed as HIV positive. She works on the street every night from anything between 6.30 p.m. until 7.00 a.m.

In my opinion she is a hazard to society. She injects in her groin, her clothes are constantly covered in blood – and puss, from her sores. I have reported this to her probation officer, and still no one really seems bothered. Do you think it's right that she could be infecting at least ten punters per night with the HIV virus? Services offered out on the street can be as low as £5.00! Safe sex isn't a priority or an option for a drug addict who's desperate for money. It's not even a consideration if the punter wants unprotected sex. There are no laws which protect society against what she is doing ...

When I collect my daughter's washing I handle everything with gloves. You never know what you're going to find. Quite regularly I find condoms, crack pipes and needles floating around in my washing machine.

In the last 12 months my daughter was abducted by a punter and taken to an industrial unit. This was reported to the police, but, of course, no charges were ever brought against the man.

She has been attacked by vigilantes out on the street; held down on the floor by two men, beaten up, and she would have been raped if someone hadn't responded to her screams. Most recently, a punter just pulled up in a car and poured diesel all over her. There could be an awful lot more that I just don't know about.

As a parent it's your worst nightmare. I work in the centre of a town where the men who work for my company regularly see my daughter on the street on their way to work. The humiliation is unbearable, but more annoying is the fact that when she goes to court for prostitution she receives nothing more than a fine. So far this year she has been in front of the magistrates at least ten times.

My daughter and her pimp/boyfriend live with his mother in a one-bedroom warden-controlled, old person's property. They're both injecting addicts, and both HIV positive. They live in squat conditions in her living room. I've reported this to the local council, social services, probation officer and drug worker; still no one will take steps to change this situation.

What would you do if this were your daughter? Who would you turn to for help? I have found that there are many definitions of the word 'pimp'. My daughter's pimp is her boyfriend, lover and co-dependant. Of the many girls working out on the street today, the majority are feeding their own addiction or supporting their pimp's drug habit – or both. What is the government doing about this? They don't have any answers for this type of problem.

In a recent telephone conversation with my daughter's probation officer, the only advice he could give me was: 'You get on with your life, and let your daughter get on with hers.' But my daughter has no life, by any definition of the word 'life'.

I don't think my daughter will live to come out of this situation. I fear that any change in the law will be too late for her. It feels as if I am watching my daughter die in front of my eyes. I am completely helpless.

What I've been saying isn't fiction. It's fact. I live daily with the fear that I could be a phone call away from her death.

We all stand here in front of you with horror stories to tell, and these will continue unless there are drastic changes in our laws.

Please listen to what we are telling you. At the moment this is only my story. It could quite easily become my daughter's obituary.

The constructive use of shame: a reflection on John 8.1–11

It is a grim narrative; a nameless, voiceless, defenceless woman surrounded by her accusers. She is presumed guilty and condemned.

Her accusers are using her to get at Jesus: they play off the words of Moses against him ('Thou shalt not commit adultery'), trying him out, searching for some accusation against him; wanting a response to their suggestion that they stone her. He plays for time (at least, that is one way of interpreting his actions), by stooping down to trace his finger on the ground.

Can we imagine this woman and Jesus himself? The one is confronted by accusers, the other rightly wary of a trap; both likely to suffer not merely verbal but physical intimidation, and their silent prayer to God for deliverance from evil.

This nasty little scene is staged somewhere in the temple precincts with many people present, many of them being taught by Jesus. His teaching is disrupted by the deliberate bringing in of 'a woman taken in adultery' – goodness knows what had happened to the man involved!

So far as we know, Jesus had never met the woman before and had no idea who she was, how she lived, where she came from, how she had been caught. Perhaps she was not married – where was her husband if she was? Perhaps a widow? Perhaps starving and selling sex for cash? Perhaps with hungry children to feed? Might she even be a stooge for a set-up confrontation? We will never know.

Whoever she is, Jesus stands by her and sees off her accusers. (We might recall at this point some of his words from Matthew 5.28: 'Whosoever looketh on a woman to lust after her hath already committed adultery with her already in his heart.') In this pronouncement he goes further than her accusers. His point is that what goes on in the heart matters very much. If it matters how we think of one another, imagine our relationships with one another, then Jesus is turning the tables – both in the theoretical passage in Matthew and here, in the temple, in practice.

He says, 'He that is without sin among you, let him first cast a stone at her.' He convicts them by appealing to their own consciences. The oldest (perhaps the wisest and most honest) leave first.

After Jesus has 'seen off' the woman's accusers, we hear a brief interchange between Jesus and the woman; alone together in this very public place. Has no one condemned her? She replies, 'No man, Lord.' He tells her that he does not condemn her either, but urges her to leave and to sin no more.

At the very least, we can learn one thing from this: there is judgement of *who we are* as well as of what we do.

This passage is so vivid that you can consider yourself to have been a witness to this frightening event. *You* saw it. *You* were there. *You* heard it all. How do you react? What will you do? Are you blind, deaf, voiceless? Perhaps you feel as helpless and overwhelmed as that nameless woman. Perhaps you are still playing for time – even though Jesus has shown you what to do.

We can learn from this passage to shape our imaginations. To cultivate sympathy and understanding of others, so we can stand by them; *especially* when we think, or indeed *know*, that they have done terrible things.

Please, however, make the distinction between reserving judgement on others and believing that anything goes. Of course we must always separate out what we know is good, better, best from what is bad, worse and worst. We need to stay aware at all times of our own ability to be downright wicked.

Now let's turn back to Jesus' brief exchange of words with the woman. He urges her to sin no more. Let us not fall into the trap of believing that his words mean that she actually had committed adultery. But what else could his words mean? Let me quote some words of the great nineteenth-century reformer Josephine Butler on this passage, words written in 1869, as she was about to launch her campaign against her own society's disgraceful treatment of women.

> She wrote of Christ:
>
> In one case He emancipated a woman from legal thraldom: His act no doubt appeared to those who witnessed it as that of a dangerous leveller; for while He granted to the woman a completeness of freedom from the tyranny of law which must have electrified the bystanders, He imposed upon the men present, and upon all men by implication, the higher obligation which they had made a miserable attempt to enforce upon one half of society only, and the breach of which their cruel laws visited with terrible severity on women alone; they all went out convicted by conscience, while the woman alone remained free; but, be it observed ... free in a double sense, free alike from the inward moral slavery, and from the harsh, human-imposed judgment.
>
> *(Josephine Butler (ed.),* Women's Work and Women's Culture *(London: Macmillan, 1869), p. lviii)*

There is something important here which Josephine Butler spotted and which we may easily overlook – that point about being free from 'inward moral slavery'. What she means here, I believe, is the woman's enslavement to the commonly held perception that she was worthy only of the treatment she was getting: i.e., dragged along, abused, used, accused, threatened, despised.

There is, for me, something hugely important to learn from this gospel.

You may already have anticipated what I'm going to say – which is, think about those murdered young women in Ipswich in 2006. *Of course* human judgement must be brought to bear on their *killer.* In our society, there will be a lot of effort put into understanding what makes *him* behave the way he does.

But will we put as much effort into imagining the lives and predicaments of the women he murdered? They will not be the first or the last to end up on the streets. There will be many more who become vulnerable to predators of one sort or another.

It is far, far too easy to think that somehow these women deserved what they got. It is far too simple to attribute their weaknesses and vulnerability to their dependence on drugs etc. But somewhere in that reasoning, isn't there an issue about their own responsibility for their lives? Did they not think that they deserved better? Why?

Rather than blame, we need to use what we might call the *constructive use of shame*; the kind of shame which, eventually, made the woman's accusers turn away, chastened by their own admittance of sin. Except with one significant difference: just suppose even one of her accusers or one of the onlookers had acknowledged his shame, and then remained behind and said, 'Now what can I do to help here?'

Or, in our own case: 'Who can I support who is directly involved in helping to fight such use and abuse of vulnerable people, many (though not all) of them girls and women?'

That would be a constructive use of our *own* shame.

© Ann Loades

Dog-girl

When you are a dog,
You watch your master all the time.
If he comes close
I look at the ground.
If he strokes you
You are happy it is not a beating.

Dogs cannot think.
Thinking is not for dogs.

When you are a dog
You obey straight away.
Come here.
Lie down.
Roll over.

If you are good
You get to eat and to sleep.

If I am not good
He beats me with
The lead from the kettle.

This is all a dog can expect.
I am a dog now.

There is a little park
Away through the alley
Which my window looks down through.

Dogs run there, no leads, playing.

But I am frightened of sticks.

© Lucy Berry

Chaste

Over his shoulder the dado flowers
stretch like hems of cornfields near Tartu – ow –
that I garlanded as summer's green man
hung over me in an oak tree. Never
another blue cloud-pearled sky, just myself
and wallpaper making the world a dream.

Maybe the ceiling's the place where a dream
comes true, opens into sky and flowers
raining their colours. I cover myself
with petals and my skin is a rose – ow –
the ceiling drops barbed wire and I never
struggle free, each wire barb is every man

who tears my soul because he's not a man
but the sky falling in. I used to dream
in cornfields, spread out at the sky, never
closing my eyes because the blue flowers
were my eyes in the wheat, the barbed wire – ow –
in the hedge I decorated myself

I covered with leaves, and I leave myself
lying under the sky, before the man
lied. That was then. That was my self. I – ow –
pluck at the hem of my skirt in the dream,
the stiff red skirt embroidered with flowers
that I wore in the fields, that I'll never

wear again, see again. And I'll never
wash these new clothes enough to feel myself
fit to lie down among sky-clean flowers.
The ceiling, the door, the lock is a man
with barbed wire round my neck. If I could dream
I'd dream of a middle-aged woman – ow –

lying on her back in a wheat field – ow –
with field-mice, birds and rabbits and never
any men, and arching blue flowers dream
above her in the clouds. Come to myself
in this room, in this town, under this man
whose breath's putrid as rotten cut flowers.

I must remember – ow – my name, my self.
I wish I had never. One smiling man
sold me a dream. I'll die without flowers.

Her Valentine

I want a pink card
With a quilted-silk heart
And 'Be My Valentine' in red.
And sweet printed words of love inside
For the cut on the side of my head.

I just need a bunch
Of some pretty bright flowers
Or a bottle of fizz works like a charm
And 'Be My Valentine' in my ear
To forget this big bruise on my arm.

He's broke my nose twice.
Look it's crooked, you see?
But we made it up quite quick, that time.
He's not so bad after all is he?
If he always buys me a Valentine?

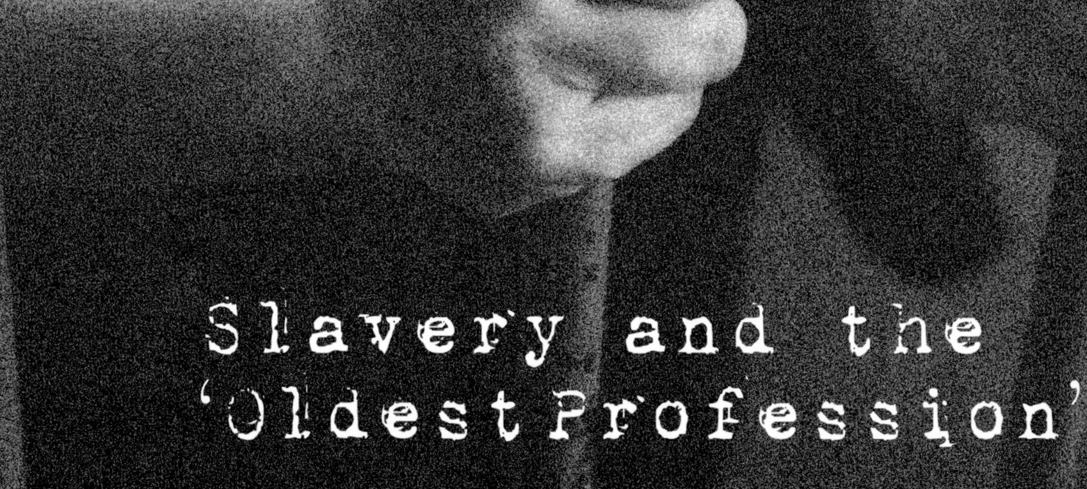

Slavery and the 'Oldest Profession'

Remember them that are in bonds, as being bound with them. Even if we lack the sympathy which makes us feel the chains which bind our enslaved sisters, we cannot escape the fact that we are one womanhood; we cannot be wholly and truly free.

Josephine Butler

Profession? What profession?

Prostitution is not the oldest profession – it is no profession at all. What kind of profession is it when the longer that you stay within it, the worse your health is, the more at risk all your life circumstances become? What kind of profession is it which few mothers, fathers or teachers would want children to enter, mindful of those children's future well-being and happiness? In what other profession are its members beaten, reviled, kidnapped and often murdered?

This is no profession. Prostitution is the most profound and invasive form of exploitation from the beginning of the journey to the end. The grooming, enticements, deception and abuse practised in its 'career development' are the grossest form of betrayal. Having one's body purchased for money is a profound denial of our divine gift of equality and dignity. For men and women, punter, pimp and prostitute, human dignity is eroded. For those trafficked into prostitution this is no 'professional opportunity' but violent enslavement into the contemporary slave trade for sex.

The bleeding obvious: slavery and salvation in the Bible

Two hundred years after the Abolition of the Slave Trade Act, we still have slavery. It's a regular trade that tricks, buys and kidnaps women in order to service men who want sex without relationship.

We don't call what goes on today 'slavery', of course. We talk instead about 'the sex industry'. We don't talk about slaves, either: we talk about 'whores', 'prostitutes' and 'sex-workers'.

Look how cunning we're being in resisting the language of slavery and using these sorts of words instead. If we call enslaved women 'whores' or 'prostitutes', we absolve ourselves of moral responsibility for them. They're slappers – criminals. They're indecent. They're sub-human – after all, they're for rent! They don't deserve our care or protection. They're commodities – bodies for sale.

But if we face the fact that they're *slaves*, we have to do something about them, because slaves need and warrant liberation. Their enslavement in the sex industry is then something that is done *to* them. And then we have to face a responsibility.

Why is it that slavery is something we recognize only with great difficulty and reluctance – and usually only retrospectively? What *is* it that makes it so easy to miss the 'bleeding obvious' – that predisposes us to believe the obscuring lies we tell ourselves?

We did it with the 11 million slaves from Africa. They were, of course, black. We told ourselves that this made them sub-human in a hierarchical pyramid in which 'human' was defined by whiteness. We graded all other people of colour according to their distance from the white apex.

'We're not as naive any more,' we protest. 'We know that people of colour are as human as we are. We've come a long way from the racist theories of the past!'

But actually, we didn't enslave black people because they are black and because we were prejudiced. We enslaved them for economic reasons – we had the *ability* to enslave them, and we needed slaves as a source of cheap labour.

It was this fear that generated our racism. It led to theories about the genetic inferiority of black people, so that enslaving them and treating them as sub-human beasts was not only justifiable, it was both necessary and a duty!

What's my point here? It's a simple one: slavery is an evil thing, and when we get involved in evil, we look for ways to justify ourselves. We won't look honestly at it as *our* problem.

It's happening again now with today's slaves – the women in the sex trade – over morality. We're justified (in our own eyes) in tolerating the evil done to these women, because our terminology has turned them from oppressed slaves into 'immoral whores' who have *chosen* to rent themselves out for use and abuse!

In the same way that we ignored the unspeakable treatment of the black slaves, we now ignore the fact that these women are not free agents, but victims of their own desperation and of deceit, abuse and rape.

For an institution that sets such public store by sexual probity, the Church is remarkably susceptible to being seduced from its primary task: to incarnate, live and preach the Good News of God's salvation for all creation.

We've always been like this, haven't we? Slavery has a particular power to distract us from salvation. What makes us so blind and deaf to the plight of these human victims of our greed and evil? *Why* did it take so long for the Church to wake up to this evil?

Why wasn't the Church (rather than a few courageous individuals within it) at the forefront of the abolitionist movement?

If we want to understand structural (or systemic) sin, we need to look at how our participation in – or tolerance of – slave-trades distorts our reading of Scripture.

We're used to arguments about black people being descendants of Ham and therefore destined by God to be 'hewers of wood and drawers of water'. We now see these arguments for the racist rubbish that they are. Less 'quaint' are the debates about what the Bible does and doesn't say about the institution of slavery: if slavery is so evil, why do Jesus and Paul (for example) not condemn it?

But why were we prepared even to engage in these debates over the slavery issue? How could any Christian even *begin* to try and justify the institution of slavery from the biblical texts?

I ask this because liberation from slavery is the key image of salvation in the Bible. To *be* 'Israel' is to be the community that owes its existence to the God who liberates the slaves. To be Yahweh is to be the God of Compassion and Liberation – the God who hears the groans emanating from the brick-pits of Pharaoh and who acts to free them. To be 'mighty' is to be the God who performs the acts of liberation – who defeats the armies of the slave-owning empire represented by Pharaoh. Yahweh's triumph is seen in the dead horses and soldiers of the pursing Egyptian army (the slave-owners) whom Yahweh drowns.

When we read Exodus – that great liberation – we are breathing the air that the biblical writers breathe when talking about God's saving acts. Exodus is the dominant image of salvation.

Centuries later, in 587 BC, Jerusalem was destroyed and Judah was taken into exile. It is an enormous crisis. The people's faith was shattered: Yahweh had promised that Jerusalem would never fall and that Yahweh would always be with them. The Exile shattered those beliefs. The prophets turned to their history to re-understand God all over again. And look what happens: the Exile is cast in terms of re-enslavement in Egypt, and the promise of Return (under Cyrus in 538 BC) as the New Exodus.

Six hundred years later, the Roman occupation was understood religiously and theologically through the lens of continuing bondage in Egypt/Babylon.

Freedom from bondage is therefore the image which Jesus chooses to describe his mission and ministry in the synagogue in Luke 4. Mark, similarly, presents Jesus chaining the Strong Man and unchaining his slaves.

But, contrary to expectations, Jesus doesn't just come to save Israel. God is acting in Jesus to save all of created reality. The cosmic drama of salvation that the New Testament writers portray is the story of a cosmic battle between God and Satan – between the Enslaver of the World and the World's Liberator. God's reign is a reign of freedom and will bring freedom for a world presently in chains.

Now the godless obscenity of Christians' involvement in slavery becomes clear: how can slave-trading and slave-owning be, in biblical terms, anything other than to ally ourselves with Pharaoh, with Babylon, with Rome and with Satan?

How did our Christian forebears miss this? How could good Christian people, genuinely seeking to be faithful to God in Jesus Christ, become involved in such evil – and then seek to justify it biblically and theologically?

The answer to this question is devastatingly simple. If you are in the slavery business, you dare not read the texts about liberation from slavery as relevant to *this* world, because you'd have to be opposed to slavery, not involved in it! So you spiritualize them, by making salvation refer only to the hereafter.

But if you subscribe to this 'spiritual' notion of salvation, life is robbed of meaning. If there is no actual liberation, then there is no 'mighty God' – no Deliverer – who can take on the powers that enslave human beings in every possible sense.

If that is true, then (a) small wonder we have concentrated on legal ('forensic') models of atonement (pictures of guilty prisoners standing before God the Judge in the divine court). If God doesn't save *this* world, (b) this so-called god with whom we end up is a much smaller god than Yahweh, the God and Father of our Lord Jesus Christ.

This mini-god is a punk. The best he (and this is very definitely a divinely challenged 'he-god') can do is rescue the few people who can be persuaded to follow Jesus and pin their hopes on heaven, and then nuke the rest of creation in a fit of pique. He can annihilate creation – but he can't save it!

That was Karl Marx's gripe about the Christianity of his day. It justified oppression and kept the workers enslaved to their cruel capitalist masters by promising them a brighter future in the hereafter; the means of making slaves comfortable with their chains.

If we, as followers of Christ, tolerate slavery or oppression then Karl Marx, or any trenchant atheist, or simply any decent human being who struggles to change the world, and who succeeds in liberating captives, is more compassionate and more powerful than the God who delivered up Jesus for our sin and raised Jesus from the dead for our salvation.

That's the sort of blindness that being involved in – or being tolerant of – slavery brings. It's the blindness which is a feature of structural sin. Instead of being heralds of the Good News, we become part of that from which the world needs saving.

No wonder the Church is in such a mess. We should be facing the hard fact that the Church has lost its way. It has lost sight of the gospel – the astounding story of our God's determination to save and transform this world into the Kingdom of God. How did we do something so extraordinarily careless and destructive? More importantly, how can we protect ourselves against it happening again?

All this is isn't difficult. It's not about deep theology or complex social theory. We need to read the Bible again – but open-eyed this time, recognizing how we've shut ourselves off from the bleeding obvious: *when the biblical writers speak about salvation, they mean, first and foremost, something that's relevant for this world. Christian faith is about what happens in the hereafter – but only because it first happens in the here and now!*

If we do this we will begin to see the desperation and agony of the women who are in chains today. We will see them as human beings. We will comprehend and despise the lies that we've told ourselves about them. We will understand that their liberation is God's cause and our mission.

There's no short cut. We mustn't get lost as before. Until we actively struggle to end slavery in *our own time*, the message of salvation is not Good News for us. It is Good News to slaves; it is Bad News to Pharaoh, Babylon, Rome, Satan and slavers.

Body and soul together

What is my body but water and blood?
All bits and pieces of lumps and bumps.
Quenched by wine
Warmed by clothes
Starved by money
Fed on food.

What was my soul but chuckle and sigh,
Quips, prayers, a bawdy drinking song?
Quenched by love
Starved of love.
Lost in a crevice of body-gone-wrong.

Keeping body and soul as one
As I got thinner day by day
Hunger gnawed at my body and so
Made me choose the only way.

The only way to keep them one:
I lay on my back in this empty room
Pretending the Virgin over again
To this, that, the other ugly groom.

My soul is long from my body now.
How shall I survive forever the lack?
There is no bread and wine in me
Just ugly crumbs I earn on my back.

What was my soul?
It was chuckle and sigh.
I feel it gone. I feel it gone.
I feel so little nowadays.
Lost in a crevice of body-gone-wrong.

Mariana

The words come tumbling out:
She says she is heavy with child.
She has died, yes, she says she has died.

She says: 'Who am I? I find myself only when I look out,
Up there, on the ceiling, out there ...
Here I do not exist – it is too, too painful to exist as me.

'I died at the age of seven.
He lay on me and abused me, my Father.
I kept looking at the ceiling
When he came into my room
And pretended I was there on the ceiling.
Not here, in this bed, with him.

'Later on,
Trafficked to be the chattel of thirty men a day,
I continue to be dead.
Not me –
Another – surviving the pain.
I am left alone on the ceiling.
I have died.

'Who am I?'

'Now I have escaped from the men,
I have colluded with the officials.
They laugh at me, ridicule me, say I am mad.
They use my information and give me nothing.
I smell, I am unclean, I am with nothing.
I am nobody.

'Take my baby, give it a life.
I have died.
I cannot love.
I am frozen inside.
I am lost.

'Will somebody give me back my life?

'Will anybody care enough to listen?
To keep listening
To keep listening
To keep listening ...

Let's bust some lazy assumptions about prostitution

1 **'Prostitution has always been with us – it always will be.'**
NO! In the beginning was the Word – and the Word was with God. Was Woman created as commodity to Man? We do not believe so.

2 **'Prostitution prevents rape.'**
NO! Prostitution is rape; rape in which our culture and our society currently collude. Sweden believes this so vehemently that it recently changed its legislation to prosecute those who pay for sex.

3 **'Men will always buy sex to meet their sexual needs.'**
NO! *Some* men will always *try* to buy sex. There are loads of men who want to have sex only with someone whom they are in happy relationship with. Second, that some men buy sex does not indicate some gender-disparity of sexual need. It merely indicates a disparity of power.

4 **'Men who use prostitutes are white, lonely and single.'**
NO! Research shows that paying for sex is *more* common among men who have sexual partners. All prostitutes will tell you that the men who use them are all colours – and all religions.

5 **'Everyone has the choice whether to become a prostitute.'**
NO! If you have no alternatives, prostitution is not a choice. For many women, including those who have been trafficked, choice never enters into it.

Please, if you hear anyone airing these kind of views, point out the reality ...

Love's not for sale

You heard a voice cry out
Look the other way,
I'm not a face you see,
You don't see my chains
I want to be secure
I want my own front door
Came for security
But now they're killing me

Pink glow suffused the hall
Another stranger calls
I'm not the name they see
I'm not a human being
Here in these modern chains
Caged by a wrong desire
I'm just a piece of fuel
Stoking their raging fire

I need some love

Creature of the night
I wasn't meant to be
Used, confused, abused, by those that surround me
I never had a voice
I never had a choice
Stuck in the chains we made
I'm a modern slave

I want to know I'm heard
You need to tell my tale
They need to know right now
That I am not for sale
I wanna feel secure
I want my own front door
Stuck in these chains they've made
I'm a modern slave.

When morning comes it's bright
I've been out all the night
I can almost believe this isn't real.
I want my freedom,
I want my life, love to be free,
I'm here in chains, modern day slave
My love's not for sale.

Grey shadows

I expect there are many mice
In these old houses,
Living behind skirting boards
Or under the floor,
Playing out short lives
In half-light,
In fear of heavy footsteps.

Shy grey shadows,
What have you to do with me?

I turned the corner,
By the tobacconists, at dusk
And my eye was drawn upwards,
Caught by pink blossom
Over a rusting shed.

At a high window, framed in blossom,
Back-lit by one bare bulb,
Was the shadow of a girl.

Before I could raise my hand,
It turned away into the room
For fear of heavy footsteps.

What have you to do with me?

Professional qualifications

Where will she work?
Number Eight; the one with no window.

She'll put in how many hours?
Until I let her stop.

How will she work?
Whatever way they want.

Is she lippy?
She doesn't speak the language.

Has she had any experience?
None whatsoever.

She sounds perfect.

Personal reflection on Exodus 1.15–21

The story of the Exodus – the escape of the Hebrews from Egypt – is the classic Scripture story, which has inspired many groups and peoples to escape from persecution and slavery. It describes the beginning of the Hebrews' journey from Egypt to their Promised Land. It has inspired them ever since, recited Passover after Passover.

It is a story which inspired the African slaves of the sugar plantations to seek their freedom. It also inspired black South Africans as they sought freedom from Apartheid.

Women seeking ordination in the Church of England used it, during their years on the margins. It formed the centre of many a wilderness liturgy.

Moses, who led the children of Israel out of Egypt, might never even have survived infancy except for the passive civil resistance of the Hebrew midwives Shipnah and Puah. They refused to obey the command of Pharaoh to kill all the Hebrew baby boys and made the excuse that, by the time they got there, the birth was over and the baby boy hidden away. They took a tremendous risk.

So often it is women who show the first initiative and start movements for freedom.

Hannah Moore was prominent in the anti-slavery movement. Josephine Butler took on the Establishment seeking justice and health-care for women prostitutes.

It was the Methodist Women's Network which kept pressing and pressing Downing Street with petition after petition until the law was changed so that British men can now be prosecuted for paying to have sex with children in countries such as Thailand.

It is women who have been in the van of the movement to stop sex-trafficking; and to provide care for those who have been trafficked. In England, the women of CHASTE and other organizations devote themselves to changing the attitude of the churches and the lives of the women concerned. In Scotland women of the Ecumenical Forum of European Christian women have worked hard on this issue and obliged the Scottish Parliament to take sex-trafficking seriously.

We must all be ready to work and to pray; to be midwives of new freedom and new hope for those caught up in that terrible slavery ...

O loving God,

our Creator, Redeemer, Sustainer and Friend,
we thank you for the courage and example of brave women
who have pioneered movements for justice and liberation.
Be near to all who suffer grievously as a result of sex-trafficking.
Help those who try to give them new freedom and fresh dignity.
Stir the hearts of those in authority to provide just laws and safe havens.
Convict and convert those who profit from this terrible industry.
Give life and hope to those who want a new beginning.
We ask this in the name of Jesus,
who in his earthly life treated women with respect and with dignity.
Amen.

Rahab's lament (Joshua 2.1–24; 6.22–25)

They have gone, the foreign soldiers,
Not desiring this time the ravishing of my spent flesh,
But seeking deeper betrayal; my people, my children,
In service of their god's quest.

And, Oh, my children, who are you?
Where are you?
What have I done to you?
What is left of me, once fair and becoming;
famous, like the Beloved of their Song of Songs?
See in these ageing lines around a once-beauteous face,
these sunken eyes, with shamèd depths,
these withered breasts, too roughly fondled, oh,
far too many times;
a long memory of struggle for you, my small loved ones ...

Once the child-bride to a warring chieftain of this land:
he was rough but kindly and I bore him three sons,
before his death in battle.
They left to carry on his fight.

A penniless widow has little choice...
Even beggary's denied her, when the land suffers drought and famine.
Your body, they said, your only chance, if 'you seek life'.
What does this mean?

Here in this lonely spot, the stranger comes,
seeking bread and board,
and sometimes more, the solace of the soul.
As for me – soulless ecstasy, shameful fumblings,
the mind transcending endless groping.
And then, the child, my joy.

Sometimes black from Ethiopian soil, you were,
or from Phoenician shores.
My neighbours grew jealous:
they forced themselves on me.
'This foreign brood', they jeered.
'It's sons of the land, we need, not daughters.'

Oh, my loves, I failed you.
You in your turn were taken for this cruel trade.
Your pleading eyes still haunt me
and forever will.

Forgive me, my children darlings, that to feed you,
I dressed this ageing body in dazzling clothes,
draped my neck with jewels,
prepared wine ... and aroused the appetite of
new arrivals in this land
and local chieftains equally.
I see your little, saddened faces huddled against the wall,
trying to sleep.

And now they come, these emissaries from an alien god.
What do they really want?
With aching heart I tell them what they ask,
to save my father's house.

What have I to lose, having lost all?

Conquer the land, they shall,
but they will not bring you back.
There is no balm for such deep grief ...

From Schipol to Amsterdam Central

It is a Sunday in December
And I am visiting friends in Leiden.
Tomorrow is Sinte Klaas, the festival of children.
The Zwarte Piets hand tiny biscuits to shoppers
And dance to a barrel organ beside the canal.
As light fades, we're on to Amsterdam.
Happy, I settle in my seat on a clean Dutch train
Which departs in silence and exactly on time.

At Schipol, more passengers, fresh from flights.
I notice the man first, talking on a mobile phone.
What language is that? Greek? No. Is it Russian?
His face, reflected in the train window is heavy,
Blunt-featured with shaggy brows; almost brutal.
Instinct warns me and I drop my gaze,
Pretending to read, but too late;
He has seen me, thinks maybe I am listening.

He lowers his voice, but I comprehend nothing.
Well, not yet. Then I see her. Then I understand.
Her face looks old for her age, mouth lined by smoking.
She is plastered with old-fashioned, orange make-up;
Has crude nail and hair extensions; cheap, tight clothing.
She speaks to a tall man sitting across the aisle;
It seems the three of them are together.
He toys with a cigarette, then replaces it in the packet.

He looks more like a business man,
But the hard, dead eyes give him away.
Is her passport stowed in his pocket by now?
She is animated, talks a lot, looks confident, brazen.
Have they paid a handsome price for this one?
Or perhaps she is herself a trafficker, one of the gang;
Experienced and too old for the game;
A Judas Goat luring girls to be snared.

The slave girl: reflections for the Seventh Sunday after Easter (Acts 16.16–25)

This slave girl had probably been captured during imperial expansion. War, annexation, globalization, all these make women, men and children vulnerable to capture by incoming power-brokers. Adam Smith, commenting on the trans-Atlantic slave trade, wrote this:

> The pride of man makes him love to domineer, and nothing mortifies him so much as to be obliged to condescend to persuade his inferiors. Wherever the law allows it, and the nature of the work can afford it, therefore, he will generally prefer the service of slaves to that of freemen.

Symptoms of abuse, neglect and dehumanization, which Smith abhorred, are present in sex-slavery today. The 'pride of man' still inclines many to domineer, preferring the service of slaves to that of an evolving relationship with a free woman.

The slave girl – used for the private gain of her 'owners' – is forced to tell the fortunes of those who passed by; pimped by others for her gifts of foreknowledge. Those who consult her on their way to worship, business, home, have no regard for her condition. Her 'owners'' only interest is profit as they set her to work each day.

Paul and Silas eventually recognize her bondage. 'Very much annoyed', Paul breaks the cycle of her abuse by liberating her from her skill as fortune-teller. With it her journey to freedom begins. What will her former owners do as retribution? Where will she stay and earn her living? Can she return to her homeland and loved ones? These big questions are left unanswered. The focus remains on the fate of Paul and Silas and their missionary breakthrough in Philippi; the conversion of the Philippian jailer.

Where women are caught today in prostitution (and there are, in the UK alone, over 80,000 women either caught in the market for pay-as-you-go sex or enslaved), our culture condones 'ownership' and 'client use', exploitation and pay-as-you-go-abuse of another. We await the rising up of a spirit of outrage similar to Paul's.

We have police forces, social services, health services, lawyers and churches to provide the liberating power, but not (yet) the tasked budgets. We have the ability but not (yet) the political will. We have the ability but not (yet) the legislation to protect liberated slaves as they seek sustainable ways into individual futures; as they undergo painful, slow exodus.

We have the ability but not yet the word of *all* the churches (against which the power of Hades cannot prevail), to say 'Enough! Let the slave girl go free! Break the power of demand! Let women, men, children live in equality and respect!'

Thankfully, the forces of law and order are unlikely to imprison us. But those who work in this area often face menace and aggression while confronting and undermining 'owners' and potential clients.

Paul and Silas acted locally in the city of Philippi. Their 'interference' promoted the Church's growth, and the understanding of those who saw and heard them. *We* need to think and act locally, nationally and globally.

This is a message for all. We need to engage with slave-women's need for liberation in our youth work, our schools, home groups, mums' groups, men's groups, our church leadership and our outreach teams. It is one of the malign spirits of our age, which needs to be rebuked and sent packing.

Thanks be to God.

Daughters and Sisters

Am I not a man and a brother?

Josiah Wedgewood, 1807

Am I not a woman and a sister?

CHASTE, 2007

Anna – the stolen pencil

My name is Anna.
Home is far away
Beyond the pine forests,
Towards a blood-red sun
Which rises, above snow and ice,
On the pond beside our dacha.

My mother is ill.
She must not know my torment –
Must not know of the stripping violation,
Lost virginity, integrity,
The shame, my despair.

Being rescued held more shame;
That sudden exposure to light.
Needing food, shame is inescapable.

Lying in the dark, self-accused,
Wrapped in *Sin*.
That stupid word
Of childhood's faith.

Into that dark despair,
A childhood memory sparks,
Of another burning shame:
A stolen pencil.

Oh, oh, the sudden exposure to shame!
And of others' disappointment.
Just disappointment:
Oh, oh! Worse by far.

My aunt opened that door.
She opens it again now
To this shamed child.
Opens her arms.

She casts dark forces out by Love;
The impossible, made possible.

Such love, cherished in silence,
Lasts a lifetime.

No more Sin
Than the theft of a pencil.

A family's story

Sophy, the youngest of our three children, is now nearly 29. She is the mother of four children. A shy, generous, beautiful child, she embarked upon what we thought was a phase of normal teenage rebellion at the age of 13. In the blues-bars part of our city she was targeted and groomed by a man about seven years older than her. He became, as he intended, her pimp.

At 16, she moved out and her 'boyfriend' moved in with her. By 17, she was working in saunas and massage parlours, and as an escort in London and abroad. She earned huge money – £1000 to £2000 in a weekend – but it was hardly a life. I kept a journal sporadically. Here are some of the entries:

> *March 1994*
> *Saturday; woken at 8.00 a.m. by door-bell. Sophy in terrible state. At first swearing and refusing to talk. 'Shut up you bitch, you don't understand. I just want to die.' Eventually it transpired that Leo had driven her home from the sauna to her flat. Taken all her money. 'But I love him. No one else is there for me. Where are my friends this morning? Life is not worth living without him!'*
>
> *January 1996 (after her son Luke was born)*
> *As bad as ever. Last week Leo beat her up – after she seemed to manage without him for a while. She still thinks that he will give her less hassle if she does not press charges. Since then he has beaten her up, even while she was holding Luke; he has also stolen her new gold bracelet and her watch. She was in a terrible mood with me; she just kept saying we were ruining her life because we tried to control her all the time.*
>
> *May 1996*
> *I keep writing that it cannot get worse and yet it seems to do so. Last weekend was terrible. She came round asking for money for Leo for petrol. We would not give it to her. Later she came round again, saying that Leo would not give Luke back unless she paid the money. We would not give it. 'If I had 10 grand I would give it all for Luke and you will not give me £30.'*

Sophy is no longer working as a prostitute, but there isn't a simple, happy ending to the story. The effects of her experience still shape her life. She is still emotionally trapped in her teenage years; she finds it hard to trust anyone or to form adult, mutual relationships. Although underneath it all she is gentle and loving, it is highly unlikely that she will ever find a long-term caring partner. Her experiences have led her to develop a defence mechanism that prompts her to explode aggressively.

As parents, now in early 'retirement', much of our time and energy is still taken up with supporting Sophy and our grandchildren. We never planned to care full time for a grandchild, but that's what we're doing. It is not easy for Sophy to care for three children on her own. When she is stressed, we get violent verbal abuse; she knows where to put the knife in.

It isn't easy for the grandchildren; they have to learn to cope with various manifestations of the damage that was done in the past, to their mother and the whole family.

Our older daughter still feels angry about how her *own* teens were affected by what her sister was doing. Even now she feels that we allow ourselves to be exploited by Sophy. Will it ever end?

We always wanted constructive co-operation with professional agencies, and were grateful when that happened. But experience has taught us that this co-operation has to be fought for and is sometimes denied. This is because professionals are so sure of their expertise that they can't help but be paternalistic and are unable to listen.

It helps if you are determined not to be put down and excluded from discussions – *but it should not be so crucial that people know how to put their foot in the door.*

I offer you one example. An incident, perhaps the worst of all, illustrates both the good and the bad aspects of our dealings with agencies. This is a very brief synopsis. In late 1999, when Sophy's daughter Emily was three months old, her boyfriend tricked Sophy and Emily into his car and drove them to London. There he took Emily away and told Sophy she could only have her back when she had earned enough money for him.

I had hysterical phone calls from Sophy, who had been breastfeeding Emily; she was beside herself. No one knew where Emily was. Emily was three months old. I worked hard to persuade Sophy to go to the police. She didn't want to go because, she said, they would take the baby away from her. *Of course not, I said, she was not the abductor and abuser of her own baby.*

So she went to a police station. She was brought back to Leeds in a police car. And when the baby was found, she was taken away from Sophy and placed in not-always-satisfactory foster care, for a year. Why? Because Sophy was blamed for the abduction of her own child. The elusive Leo was not pursued and arrested. This was a bad, and I am glad to say, unusual example of crass, short-sighted, punitive social work.

But that's not the point I want to emphasize here. The policeman who had been overseeing the search for Emily – and who had been very supportive – said that he was so pleased there had been 'a good ending' and that Emily was safe. Of course it was wonderful that Emily was safe; but that was just a part of the total outcome which was far from being good.

Emily was kept in care for one year, away from her mother. There was a real danger that she would be taken away permanently. Recovering the baby, safe, from abduction was good, but it was not an 'ending'; for us it was the next chapter in a continuous narrative.

The policeman's pleasure at a good ending was an expression of his supportive care.

The professional imagination of the policeman was, perhaps, focused on the child alone, lost and in danger: finding the child was the key success.

The parental imagination includes the lost grandchild, *and* the baby's distraught mother, *and* the other grandchild, Luke, who might be losing his baby sister to whom he is already attached. To the professional imagination the abduction comes as news, as new information – it knows nothing of the pre-history, maybe nothing of the people involved.

Having different imaginations does not prevent co-operation. But the difference in imaginations can lead to misunderstandings, to inefficiencies and to hurt. Talking of a good ending was hurtful to me, though it did not escalate to a misunderstanding.

Over many years, (in which policemen and social workers have come and gone), we have come to the view that the institutionalized imagination of most professionals is not merely different from parental imagination, but is *profoundly resistant to it and resistant to learning from it.* In the professional imagination, parents are too often seen as part of the problem rather than as part of the solution. In parental imagination, parents can easily see themselves as secondary victims, but also as active informed agents.

Although we would have been happy to be called as witnesses, the evidence from Sophy's solicitor was cut short because the court's time was up, so Emily stayed in care for a year. We have had to work hard to be included in all the case-conferences relating to grandchildren other than Luke (who is in our care), but have probably achieved that now.

We are very persistent! But although we are present at case-conferences we have little real part in the decision-making processes. Agencies miss huge opportunities by excluding those who have become distinct experts and whose knowledge and experience can complement that of professionals valuably.

Our story is no longer the daily agony which many parents are still undergoing today. But we are still (and shall be for the rest of our lives) embroiled in the long-term effects. But I write this in the hope CROP and other organizations like it can play a part in enabling us all to work together; to change *not only systems but cultures and attitudes as well.* And that the contribution of parents can be recognized as the valuable resource that it is.

The child

She stands there so innocent,
sweet and sincere
but holds those before her in
terror and fear.

She's beautiful and tall,
full of power and strength
but inside she's shaking;
afraid to show a single tear.

She's a child,
locked away,
in an adult frame.

It seems to all that
don't know her well
that she's enjoying living
her life of hell.

But to Mum and Dad and her siblings too
she's the girl that they love.

So they continue to search,
to look for the key,
to unlock her heart
to the joy of true love
to be happy and free;

to be the child she has a right to be.

Parent Listening in the Dark

It's dark
in the distance a phone rings.

Footsteps ...
she bangs the door to.

Footsteps ...
She's gone.

It's quarter past one.

It's dark.
Can't sleep.

In the distance a phone rings.
The sound makes me weep.

Maybe this call will be the one.

She's gone.

'Get lost, Dog!'

We both recently returned from four years in Lebanon, walking where Jesus walked, and I've been reflecting on the Syro-Phoenician woman in Tyre. This story is told both in Matthew's and Mark's Gospel. It's a mother–daughter story, the story of a very sick little girl and her feisty mother ...

The woman is *desperate*. She has heard that Jesus has travelled north from Galilee; he's in town – and she immediately runs to him.

The disciples treat her the same way they treated the women who brought their children to Jesus to be blessed. Basically they tell her to get lost.

But she persists. She's a feisty one, this Greek woman, this Gentile (this 'Dog' – as Hebrew texts of the time called people like her).

She did not change her focus. She cut through all the gender-racial-cultural baggage that seemed about to block the way to her daughter's healing. She knelt at Jesus' feet. She called him 'Lord, Son of David'. She knew that all she needed was a 'crumb' from him.

And Jesus commended her faith – and the daughter was healed, immediately.

This is the kind of faith I pray you share, my beloved daughters:

A feisty faith

A focused faith.
Faith that is the door to life,
For you and yours.

© Rosemary Wallis

My three girls

There is an organized paedophile ring of men targeting young girls. I am devastated. We've gone through a three-year battle with police, CID and social services. We are still battling to get recognition that this is organized paedophile crime.

These men buy the girls gifts and make them feel special. That's the beginning of the grooming process. It is like the girls are in a cult and these men are the masters. The police say they can't do anything unless the girls make statements. But the girls are under the spell of these men! And if they step out of line they are beaten and the men threaten to petrol-bomb their houses. My daughters were made to think that these men were their boyfriends. They were just brainwashed. The things that have happened to my daughters have happened to hundreds of daughters ...

When my eldest daughter turned 13, I noticed her mood swings. I put it down to puberty to start with. She was just a normal sweet young girl who liked to do normal childlike activities. She was a very talented and outgoing child. Then in a matter of weeks I could tell she was really disturbed, but I didn't have a clue what was happening. She started coming home late, so I grounded her. I was told that a friend gave her a mobile phone. But it was the men.

I had a close relationship with my daughters and it wasn't long before she told me what was happening to her. She went missing for a couple of days and I told the police. They came round and searched my house in case I had killed her and hidden her in the wardrobe! I have had my house searched by the police 60 times.

When she came back we sat and talked and she said she went off with a man who was her boyfriend. He turned out to be 23. (At first she told me he was 18, then 21 and then I found out he was 23). She said she'd been in a house in Bradford and nothing sexual had happened. I was shocked and scared. She showed me the text messages with him saying things like 'you are my angel', 'my princess', 'you are the moon and the stars', 'I would die if I didn't have your love'. She was a 13-year-old girl who had a 13-year-old body.

About two weeks later she went out with a friend and didn't come back. It got to 1 a.m. and I got a phone call from a phone box saying they didn't know where they were and that they'd been dropped on a street. She sounded like she had been drinking so I told her to get a taxi back, which cost £20. They had been drinking a lot of alcohol – I mean a one-litre bottle of vodka. And I am not exaggerating. If the girls are still standing, the men give them more.

I never got much out of her after that. She went missing many times and wouldn't tell me anything. I would report things to police and social services so she stopped talking to me. The police told me that if my daughter was not willing to make a complaint there wasn't a crime to report. As a parent I could not do anything legally.

They said if your daughter is 13 she has to give evidence. I told my daughter I would take her to the police station but she just said that if she didn't talk there was nothing anyone could do – she knew the law better than me. It was obvious these men had told her. Our daughters are taught what to say and what *not* to say by these men.

For the next year I just had a continuous battle. These people just used her. I know that my eldest daughter went with over 60 men in the 2 years between 13 and 15.

Then my middle daughter was coming up to 13. She was asking how could her eldest sister go off with these men and why doesn't she listen to her mum? But as soon as she turned 13 her way of thinking became their way of thinking. They'd tell her that I was old and didn't want her to have any fun. They wanted her to go cruising with them and one day she got in a car. That's when I lost my second daughter.

It took them a bit longer to get her because she had seen what happened to her sister. But they made her feel so *special.* They gave her a mobile and would pull up at school at lunchtime. They get the rap music going, the drink, they smoke spliffs. They think they are Tupac and Puff Daddy. The girls are into that. And they see these men in their sports cars.

So, my middle daughter started going out with one of them. He was 19. She couldn't see she was doing anything wrong – she was doing what she was told. I talked to her about what had happened to her sister, but she just said he wasn't like that. He stayed with her for two months, then passed her to another group.

She would stay out very late and when I talked to her the following day she could hardly remember what had happened to her. I later found out her drinks were being spiked with GHB – the date-rape drug.

When she turned 15 she got friendly with a 35-year-old man. He also started seeing my eldest daughter, but neither of them knew at first. When they found out there was a massive row between them. My middle daughter went to where he worked when she found out he had been seeing her sister and went shouting at him because she was feeling hurt. He later threatened to shoot her because she had shown him up.

One night he picked her and a friend up and took them to a flat. She was given a drink and after that there was very little she could remember. She was taken upstairs and gang-raped by four men.

I heard from her friend how she had been gang-raped. She couldn't even walk afterwards. She had to go to hospital. She also had to be treated for a sexually transmitted disease. These men won't wear condoms.

I wanted to get a gun because no one was doing anything. The law couldn't protect my daughters. After that rape, they would constantly ring her, but she didn't want to know. They threatened her that they would violate me and that they would petrol-bomb the house.

Before her sixteenth birthday, she got in with an even worse group of men. They started injecting her with heroin for free because they wanted to get her into prostitution.
I was terrified she was going to die. Social services did get involved this time and she was taken to a safe place and she has been there since last October.

While I was trying to get my middle daughter into a safe place they started targeting my youngest daughter. I am so lucky with her. She has seen her two sisters go through it. She was abused by one man but luckily she didn't accept mobile phones or gifts off them. There were three times when she had sex when she was 13 with a 25-year-old; even though she had seen what happened to her two sisters, they still got to her for a while. Thankfully she doesn't want anything to do with it now.

We've had to move over 100 miles because of my youngest daughter – and my middle daughter, for when she comes out of care.

There are hundreds of men and girls involved in this. My middle daughter, in this last half-hour, has just made a list of 57 men whom she knows are involved.

My eldest daughter is now having therapy because of what happened to her.

She has now met a 24-year-old man who is married to an Asian girl. She is expecting his baby and living on her own in Keighley. She is totally in love with him and he says he is in love with her, even though he has a family. At least he is not one of this ring of paedophiles.

My middle daughter is extremely traumatized. She can't accept counselling yet. She can't face talking about it all yet. It hurts so much. She blocks everything out but it affects her every day. She lives her life scared.

My youngest daughter has not been scarred by her experiences and is doing really well at school.

I have got so much pain inside me. There has been no justice. I want parents to be able to protect their children! Why can't the parent give evidence or the child give evidence under a pseudonym so the men aren't told who it is? What kind of sick pervert can get excitement from a 13-year-old girl? They're monsters. I can't think of them as men, otherwise I couldn't be in a relationship with a man.

This is not a race thing – it's a paedophile thing. The men just happen to have dark skin. I don't want to have a Bradford riot or spark off violence. But I don't want to have to sacrifice my daughters. I should be allowed some justice.

I want the laws changed, so that parents of nine-year-old girls don't have to go through what I've been through in four years' time. The law has stopped me from being a good parent. There are laws against men grooming girls on the internet. Why not for these men who are sat outside schools in cars doing it?

Why is that not an offence?

Punters

Force always attracts men of low morality.

Albert Einstein

Trafficking: a male issue

One of two problems at the basis of human-trafficking is the men who buy these women for leisure. (The other is the poverty of women in many countries.) In order to combat trafficking, it is necessary to tackle these areas. This article will raise some questions about men's involvement and quiet support of sex as a 'human right'. It will also raise the question of whether men who buy sex should be considered as committing a criminal act.

Most men would agree that it's wrong for men to use women as slaves. However, as the market for women in prostitution differs from country to country (and because some women appear voluntarily to become prostitutes), a debate has arisen within the EU as to whether prostitution should be legalized or not. There needs to be a debate as to whether all prostitution is enslavement.

One first step is not to talk about 'voluntary' prostitutes, but to talk about prostitutes who do this 'consciously'. But there may still be some pressure behind these 'conscious' women's involvement. The mores of most of the western world reduces human beings merely to bodies which consume. Men (and especially women) are under pressure to take care of their bodies, and make them attractive. This ethos focuses on training, diet, plastic surgery, cosmetics, and so on. Bodies are big business, and the sex industry is seen as part of that business.

The debate about sexuality also reduces human beings to mere bodies – things which can be bought and sold. The fact that we human beings are spiritual is entirely lost as adverts encourage us to change our bodies. So, for us to start talking of trafficking as a *male* issue is also to begin seeing ourselves as more than simply male bodies.

To be a spiritual man is to accept that sex is more than a physical thing – it is a spiritual issue. In Germany and Holland, it is legal to be a 'sex worker'. The motivation behind this legislation is the well-being of the prostitute, who is, supposedly, given the status of 'ordinary' worker. However, in reality it is only the pimps and exploiters who gain by this easing of legalization and easier access to prostitutes.

In Sweden, it is forbidden to buy sex from another person. One reason for this ban is that experience has shown that prostitutes become victims of their past, and are exploited. Another is that most prostitution (and all trafficking) is organized by criminal networks. Swedish legislation ensures that any man who buys sex from another person is becoming, albeit marginally, part of the criminal network, supporting it financially by buying the illegal product.

So, shall *we* continue to watch men become involved in growing criminal networks by permitting them easy access to women and children? Or can we support the work that wants to make *all of this* a criminal act?

Brothel-owners want to create a greater demand for sex. The open sex market is growing. We see it advertised everywhere. The images create desire and a perceived need. At one conference I attended, the leader of a male group said that when a man sees a naked woman, his testosterone levels increase, leading to an increase in sexual desire. At the same time, the image becomes imprinted on his mind as a strong memory. It is difficult to escape such images in public areas (and on TV) in many countries. The message given to us men is, 'Even if you say no, we know what you really want!'

How do men cope with this? Making our public areas free of such images would be a good first step in the fight against trafficking and prostitution. But would that be possible? Could churches take action, for example, by refusing to buy from those companies which use such advertisements?

How can men working within the police and social services stay free from influence? To see a lot of men earning a lot of money and using women freely is, for some, a tempting situation. How is accountability monitored within these organizations? A male network with integrity can break the old habits, be of assistance for debriefing, and make other men accountable for their actions.

Most men desire to get close to women's bodies. There are many different ways for men to do this and the most common is the caring, loving, voluntary way in which there is mutual give and take. But a man may sometimes use force; taking what he wants and hitting her if she complains.

He may also use ideological, even *theological* imposition. He may tell her it is God's will that she be subordinate and obedient, and that he has rights over her. As the sociologist Manuel Castells writes: behind all fundamentalism is the urge for power – over the nation, the female body and religion.

He may use money to buy access to a woman's body for a short time. Prostitute and sex-slave are cheap to use and easy to find. He does not need to care about her afterwards. This is said to be the 'oldest profession'. It does not legitimize the deed.

There is an argument that this is the only way some men (for example, those who have physical or mental disabilities) can get sex. It is said that they *need* the opportunity to buy sexual pleasure, since they are unable to form relationships. This begs a very important question: 'Is sex a "human right"?' Is it a 'human right' to be able to buy a woman's body for my own relaxation? Such 'rights' are not mentioned in the United Nation's Declaration of Human Rights, unlike the rights not to be oppressed or enslaved. But if sex is not a human right, what is it?

What about the Bible? The Apostle Paul talks a lot about treating each other with love and dignity. He urges us not to misuse others. To buy sex from a woman is to violate that woman. It is time for us men to say that we will not support women being treated in this way.

Recently, I attended a conference in the United States on trafficking and prostitution. I heard many stories. Women from all over the world told us about their lives. My frustration grew as I heard how many men treat women.

On the final day of the conference, the men present decided to say something collectively. Some of us wrote a statement of repentance which was read out at Morning Prayer. We could not take the place of the perpetrators, but we wanted to show the women that there are men who think differently.

At this meeting we knelt before the women, who gathered round us in a prayer of forgiveness. Next to me stood a woman who had been staying in the room next to mine in the conference centre. She had never said 'hello' to me. Suddenly, she burst into tears. For a moment, we were joined together in her pain. She told me that after this, for the first time in her life, she felt really free: she could find the forgiveness to get over her hatred in the presence of men, and be free.

If men reading this wish to be seen as part of the male community which does *not* see women as things to be used, but wants to show respect and responsibility, you may wish to meditate on some of the pieces on the following pages.

Fishermen

I'm off fishing says the man.
His wife gives him a look.
He's fishing all right
with his rod, bait and hook.

He sits by the bank
and looks for his catch.
He sits by the bank
waiting for his first snatch.

He sits in his car
by the school for a while
behind windows so black
with his rap, joints and smile.

Operation Pentameter

Last year I led Operation Pentameter which involved all 55 police forces in England, Wales, Scotland and Northern Ireland. The operation was aimed at raising awareness about trafficking for sexual exploitation, and rescuing trafficking victims. The operation ran for 3 months and during that time we rescued 84 victims – 12 of whom were under 17.

British law enforcement learned a lot from that operation. We found out that the 'price' of victims differed hugely: from £8,000 for an innocent 15-year-old girl to £500 for a 39-year-old woman who'd been trafficked many times. We found that some women are forced to have sex with as many as 30 clients a day ... resulting in these organized criminals (the traffickers) making in some cases in excess of £1000 a day.

Remember, each time a man has sex with a woman who has been trafficked, *he is raping her.*

As a result of the success of Pentameter, I convinced Government ministers and police chiefs to create the United Kingdom Human Trafficking Centre – the UKHTC. The Centre is based in Sheffield. It's the first of its kind. It is a multi-agency unit working in a victim-centred approach with personnel from the Police, Crown Prosecution Service (CPS), Immigration Service, Serious and Organised Crime Agency (SOCA), Social Services, Revenue and Customs and representatives from a number of charities and other non-governmental organizations, all liaising.

We've developed new levels of co-operation between NGOs, faith communities, academic institutions and those with expertise relevant to trafficking, so that we can respond in new ways to stop trafficking: working at intelligence-gathering, the prosecution of traffickers and the protection of victims.

Since the Centre was opened, a further 66 victims of trafficking have been rescued – just between October 2006 and April 2007.

Even after all the time I've been involved in the fight against human-trafficking, I am amazed and sickened that this trade in lives and dreams still continues two hundred years after the trade in slaves was outlawed.

I feel immensely proud of what has been achieved in the last year, and in the efforts and dedication of all the people I've met who made it their business to take on the traffickers and the world of sexual exploitation. I am determined that we will make the United Kingdom a hostile environment for human-traffickers.

Chief Constable Grahame Maxwell, UK Human Trafficking Centre Programme Director

Lidia's story – Albania

The issue of human trafficking affects all countries and communities, but I'd like to tell you about one particular person – an 18-year-old girl called Lidia (not her real name) – whom I met through my work in Albanian prisons.

Lidia was arrested for the murder of two children, a crime which she told me she didn't commit. She comes from a village in northern Albania, is from a Catholic background and was the only one in the pre-detention centre who had a Bible. Lidia was very quiet, but as some of our team spent time with her, she began to tell us her story. It all began a few years ago.

Lidia was on the beach with some friends when a group of boys she knew from a nearby village came up to her and one of them asked her to go out with him. She refused and walked away. The boy persisted and then went to her father (which is the tradition in Albania if you want to date or marry a girl). Lidia's father said he went along with what Lidia wanted. This is rare in Albania, especially as this boy came from a good home and appeared to have good prospects. Again Lidia said no.

The boy was annoyed and his pride was hurt. His gang kidnapped Lidia and took her secretly to Italy. She was abused by all the gang members and then put on the streets. She was beaten if she didn't make enough money. To prevent her escaping, they often kept her in a flat and brought men to her.

Lidia was desperate to escape back to her family. She found some men who agreed to help her. While she was travelling back to Albania, the gang from which she had escaped returned to her village, looking for her. Unaware that she hadn't yet arrived back, the gang members shot her brother and injured her father. When Lidia heard what had happened she was devastated, appalled that harm had to come to her family.

The gang wanted revenge on the men who helped her escape; they put a bomb through the letterbox of one of these men's houses and his two daughters were killed. It was for these murders that Lidia was arrested.

She was taken to prison where she lived in a small cell with another five girls. The prison educators told us they thought that, even if innocent, Lidia would get a 20-year sentence; because the gang would pay the judge to avoid going to prison themselves.

We saw Lidia the day before she went to court. She asked us to pray with her. We were unsure how to pray – but we prayed that she would be strong and that God's will would be done. As we were leaving one of our team said to her, 'Whatever happens in court tomorrow, just know Jesus is with you always, so keep praying.'

We went back the following week, expecting to see her. But, the educational workers told us she had been found *not guilty* and had been released. They said it was a miracle and that she had stood up in court and said, 'Praise Jesus Christ, he has set me free.' Lidia was taken from court that day and put in hiding. We don't know where she is. A week later she phoned one of our team and said, 'I can't tell you where I am, but I'm safe and I'm praying daily to Jesus. Thank you.'

This is the last we have heard from her, but we pray she is safe. We suspect she is living in another country with a new identity.

This story – and many others like it – has challenged me to mobilize the churches here in Albania and in Europe to start addressing this issue within their communities; through prayer, prevention awareness and by supporting the victims who come into the churches for help.

Often these girls' families do not want them back. I believe it is essential that churches are ready to receive them and to help prevent this terrible form of slavery continuing.

A bit

I appreciate a bit of steak once in a while;
Something satisfying.

Most of the time I eat trash.
Does the same job.

How often can you afford a really classy girl?
Anyway, they're all the same.
Do the same job.

Nothing like a spicy bit of Thai,
If you like to travel;

Something a bit new.
Bit of a holiday.

Quiet ones who shut up,
That's what I like.
Respectful.
Young.

Plenty of it about.
If you know where to look.
Bit tasty.

A man

He likes his wife – a little.
But she goes her own way.

He dotes on his daughter
But there is no connection.
She is her mother's girl;
Since he never became a man,
They shrug him off.

He goes faithfully,
Once a week,

To a house of girls,
Where he thinks he matters.

If he wants to,
He may hit them,
Spit on them,
Shit on them.

They are the daughters of men.
He does not make this connection.

But then, he's not a man.

Groceries

There are some girls in the playground,
I know their names, we chat,
Little mums, leaning up against
The climbing frame, so tired,
Who might sell themselves for groceries.

He visits.
They go to bed.
They go to Tesco.
He buys her week's shopping.
He'll come again, some time.
It's some arrangement.

I have no judgement I could make on this.
My child does not live weeks on bread and jam;
If she can get her children chicken
And he will buy her chicken,
Even if it is not the kingdom,
I cannot call it sin.

But
There are girls who never go outside.
They have no name I know.
They have no lover.
No mother.
No shopping trips.
No outdoor clothes.
No passport.
No sin.

They *are* groceries.
The sin is the grocer's.

See me?

See me?
I believe you're staring.
I can't stop you.

See my arms?
I believe God made them
For holding tight, to family.

See my hands?
I believe God made them
For working.

See my lips?
I believe God made them
For talking.

See my legs?
I believe God made them
For walking.

See my hips?
I believe God made them
For settling a baby on.

See my breasts?
I believe God made them
For my babies and their father.

See me?
You don't.
But I can't stop you.

Time for this sort of change

We take heart from the example of Sweden, which, in 1999, introduced a law which criminalized the buying of sexual services, while those who offer sex for sale are not prosecuted. The law was part of an overall package to address violence against women, secure women's rights and diminish the likelihood of young girls entering into prostitution. The 'signal' effect of this law has been strong.

It is widely considered that trafficking for sexual exploitation has been reduced in Sweden and that there has been a considerable change in attitude among the potential male consumers. A survey on general attitudes in 2001 stated that more than 80 per cent of the population are found to be in favour of the law. About one hundred cases of violation of the law are reported each year, which are met with fines as well as imprisonment.

While there are voices who claim that on-street prostitution has become more marginalized and dangerous for those who are engaged with it, from research undertaken in Malmø it is clear that the age of those entering into prostitution is rising year on year, and that attitudes among Swedish males are clearly changing to a deeper respect for women.

Male and Female

So God created humankind in his image, in the image of God he created them; male and female he created them.

Genesis 1.27

The discipleship of equals

The discipleship of equals declared in the ancient baptismal credo of Galatians 3.28 is the heart of the Jesus movement which tore through Jewish and Gentile communities of the first century. Radical equality is declared in this baptismal announcement where there is neither Jew nor Greek, slave nor free, male nor female.

This eradication of difference allows access to God and *true* relationship to one another. No wonder that this wonderful vision, this religious programme for the overhaul of male privilege and hierarchy came so mightily unstuck in the years which separate those heady moments.

The wider mental, economic and political landscape was hostile to the memory of the discipleship of equals in anything other than its most spiritualized mode. We would be equal in heaven but not on earth.

The wonderful vision of the initial creation where God's creativity and inner equality was reflected in the creation of male and female in all the paradox of their interdependence, autonomy and mutual respect was lost.

One of the key shifts in our understanding of hierarchies, in class, ethnicity or gender, has undoubtedly been a result of the Holocaust, where a nationally championed hierarchy of ethnicity led to concerted and scientifically systemized murder. Six million Jews slaughtered in a genocide that traumatized the 'civilized leaders' of the western world for decades.

In the decades after this outrage, the Geneva Convention, the Human Rights Convention, the Convention on the Eradication of Discrimination Against Women, and the Beijing Platform have all come into being. These represent a movement which asserts human mutuality and interdependence over all forms of hierarchy.

This transformation of cultural mindset has seen the development of ideas of diversity and equality in the most systematized manner yet achieved. Yet, whatever may be happening on the national and international stages is not apparent in the domestic sphere.

If much of European legislation is beginning clearly to describe women's place as equal to men's (in employment law and property inheritance), there are still vast disparities operating behind closed doors, at home.

The Church frequently manifests this disparity. Whether you look at the Orthodox, the Roman Catholic or the Anglican Churches (to mention some of the largest Christian faith-groupings across the world), women are in a structurally subservient place. Not only in their formal articulations of liturgy. But also in the ecclesial structures, where only the male is permitted to represent God to the community, or the community to God. For only in one of those denominations are women deemed fit to be priests and in two of them neither priests, bishops nor cardinals.

The Churches must establish their own credibility. They must wrestle in engagement, prayer and study to hear the gospel of equality and liberation which reaches down the centuries. They need to wake up to the scriptural mandates in Galatians 3.28 and Genesis 1.26 where they can read so clearly that humankind – all of it! – was created in God's image and likeness.

Churches are colluding in the culture which allows prostitution, wife battering and sex-trafficking. Paul calls us to embrace radical inclusion of all races, classes, genders and abilities. It is still a scandal to use the name of Christ to refuse women's access to ecclesial leadership and theological contribution. It helps underpin the continued marginalization of women.

Churches should rejoice to be a part of the vital contemporary work of vision-shaping and building. Yet so few seem able to take their appropriate seats around the table and make their contribution, because they are (rightly) perceived by many NGOs, government bodies and activist organizations as institutionally sexist and, therefore, not in harmony with the key goals of wider national and international communities.

In the work, thinking and ministry of CHASTE, these barriers to understanding and participation are being broken down. But Churches must pay the price of their privilege in being part of this: they must stop being two-faced. They must stop manifesting oppression as well as equality.

Their public gesture must be a reordering of the Churches themselves, to the mandate of the gospel: radical equality in Christ.

Flesh like my flesh

Enslavement can take many forms, but in all its manifestations it is an extreme sign of humanity's refusal to recognize the image and opportunity of God in the 'Other'.

It is a rejection of the Divine paradigm expressed in Genesis 1–3. Adam says to Eve: 'You are bone like my bone, flesh like my flesh, mind like my mind, spirit like my spirit. In you I find what it is to be human – I find my meaning in being alive with you.'

Human beings are not only made from the same chemical stuff of the earth. They are made by God to be his ethical, responsible creatures. The potential of life is only made possible where Man and Woman are present, and recognize each other as life-bearers who must make *love*, and then nurture vulnerable, dependent new life in the wider world, sustained by the breath of God.

I remember tenderness

I remember tenderness;
My grandfather would stroke my hair
And my cheek
With cool, leather fingers.

I remember smiles;
My baby brother would smile so wide
Tiny bubbles would form
At the sides of his mouth.

I remember safety;
My father striding out to our fences
When the dogs barked
Late at night.

Good men, they were.

They are not all the same.
I must remember.

Son

Beloved little boy,
My beautiful son,
I will love you without submission.
I will adore you without worship.

You are more precious to me than my life.
But although you have all my love
You do not have all of me.

You cannot lead me into the temptation
Of believing that you count more than me.
You will never master me, my son.

Build up your soul and your mind
In tussle with me
A woman equal
To your overweening will.

Your imperious tantrums,
Flirty blackmail,
Toddler's bullying,
We will grow you out of
Before you become a man.

Male repentance: a prayer

But whenever anyone turns to the Lord, the veil is taken away. Now the Lord is the Spirit and where the Spirit of the Lord is, there is freedom. And we, who with unveiled faces all reflect the Lord's glory, are being transformed into his likeness with ever increasing glory, which comes from the Lord, who is Spirit. (2 Corinthians 3.16–18)

We men repent,
for undressing you with our eyes, for making sexual jokes and comments, and demeaning who God created you to be.

We repent,
for not giving you a safe place to experience your feminine sexuality in its God given fullness, and for not nurturing your femininity.

We repent,
for viewing pornography and seeing only body parts, rather than a person with thoughts, feelings and dreams.

We repent,
for touching you in ways you did not want, which have inflicted deep wounds.

We repent,
for making you go further than you were comfortable with.

We repent,
for believing that money gives us the right to use you, to degrade you, and then make you pretend you have enjoyed it.

We repent,
for hitting you, kicking you, beating you and not stopping,
even when you beg for mercy.

We repent,
for abusing your children.

We repent,
for raping you and violating you.

We repent,
for thinking our need for sexual release is more important than all your needs, especially your need for dignity.

We repent,
of all these things.
We accept responsibility for what we have done and we are sorry for our actions.

We repent and ask your forgiveness.

Little

Look!
Look at her little crop-top
And her little twist-skirt with the frill.
She'll break a few hearts, she will.

She gets me to paint her nails,
Bless her. It gives her a thrill.
She'll break a few hearts, she will.

For when we go out, evenings,
My friend bought her a little set
Of a little black mini-dress
And a handbag and a lipstick.
She hasn't seen them yet.

And for Christmas, her Grandma
Bought her a little pair of high heels.
She popped them on then, straight away
And said 'Now I know just how
A grown-up lady feels!'

'You've got a pretty girl there'
The two men at the bus-stop said.
'Don't I know it?' I said.
And we all said
'She'll break a few hearts, she will.'

And she giggled
And did her little disco-dance routine.

Why

because of the long drives on the motorway
talking, talking, never running out of talk

because we cooked supper together
in your tiny kitchen, and didn't fight

because of the laughter and the weeping
the jokes, the quarrels mended

because of the freedom not to try too hard
because of the urge you gave me to try harder

because I liked the me I became
better than the me I was before

because I still like myself with you
better than myself without you

because a good man is hard to find
because you are that good man

Being always in the image of God

Christian writings have often given the impression that it was Adam, and not Eve, who was uniquely created in the image of God. This seems to follow from the New Testament, and especially St Paul who drew a parallel between the first Adam, through whom all men (and women) fell, and the second Adam, Christ, through whom all may be redeemed.
Paul wrote:

> Thus it is written, 'The first man, Adam, became a living being'; the last Adam became a life-giving spirit. But it is not the Spiritual that is the first, but the Physical, and then the Spiritual. The first man was from the earth, a man of dust; the second man is from heaven. As the first man was of dust, so are those who are of the dust; and as is the man of heaven, so are those who are of heaven. Just as

> we have borne the image of the man of dust, we will also bear the image of the man of heaven. (1 Corinthians 15.45–49).

Paul is referring back to the creation story of Genesis 3 where 'Hadam' (literally, 'the earth creature') is made first, and then Eve made from his side. Paul even seemed to have some difficulty in saying that women were, in their own right, fully in the image of God. Certainly throughout historical Christianity, until modern times, human maleness was regarded as privileged in its perfection.

But the book of Genesis gives us a different picture. There we find that Genesis 3, the story of the creation of Adam and Eve, nowhere mentions the image of God. That is mentioned earlier in Genesis 1 where we read:

> Then God said, 'Let us make humankind in our image, according to our likeness; and let them have dominion over the fish of the sea, and over the birds, of the air ... God created humankind in his image, in the image of God he created them; male and female he created them, and God said to them, 'Be fruitful and multiply ...'. (Genesis 1.26–27)

These two striking verses suggest that it is male and female, either both or together, who image the beauty of God – woman cannot be effaced for we do not have the imaging unless both are present.

For a fuller Christian account of the image of God one needs to add to Genesis the famous New Testament saying of Jesus:

> 'You shall love the Lord your God with all your heart, and with all your soul, and with all your mind. This is the great and first commandment. And a second is like it, You shall love your neighbour as yourself.' (Matthew 22.37–39)

This is one of Jesus' most important teachings and draws immediately upon Old Testament teachings. Theologians have long noted its apparent incompleteness for we are told to love God with all our heart and to love our neighbours as ourselves, but not told how to love ourselves. St Augustine suggests that this is implied – we must love ourselves as we truly are, which is 'made in the image of God'. Men may have failed to see that women are (as much as men are themselves) reflections of the divine. But women too have not been taught to love womanliness in themselves, nor other women as reflecting the divine image.

Together these two teachings from Genesis and the Gospels amount to a powerful prohibition of the abuse and oppression of women. To abuse a woman, to exploit her as a commercial item within the sex industry, is to abuse the God in whose image she is made. But more, these texts provide a basis on which we can say that the glory of a woman is not destroyed or even, in the deepest sense, damaged by what befalls her if she is so unfortunate as to be raped, trafficked or abused.

Jewish thinkers have observed that, even after the eating of the apple in the Genesis story, human beings remain in the image of God; Genesis 9 gives this 'likeness' as the basis for the prohibition of murder.

A woman or girl is always in the image of God, no matter what befalls her. There can be no justification, within this frame of thought, for rejecting or killing a woman who has 'dishonoured' herself or her family, She remains the image of God, and must be reverenced as such by others and, importantly, by herself.

Justice and Us

It is the job of thinking people not to be on the side of the executioners.

Albert Camus

The spirituality of slaves

The spirituality of slaves is, naturally, the same as yours or mine. It is as strong as the individual and her experiences allow it to be. It is the vessel of great hope, joy and connection; and it as tenderly vulnerable to abuse.

We are very aware in our encounters with sex-trafficking that it is not just a woman's body which has been abducted, tortured and raped – but also her soul.

Often, the more religious the woman, the more open she is to manipulation and guilt. Among those who have been trafficked from West Africa, there are a number of specific (and bogus) 'religious' rituals to which women have been forced to submit. They function to 'seal' trafficking transactions. They take the form of curses which the victims believe will come to pass if they try to run away – or fail to pay back the money 'owed' for their transportation abroad – or seek to contact state authorities in any way.

These curses may seem primitive and irrational, but for the young women concerned they are potent and real obstacles which prevent them from seeking freedom, safety and justice. The rituals pertaining to many who come from Nigeria entail the extraction of head and pubic hair, clippings of nails and often menstrual blood, and the torment of worry placed on the concerned woman about her ability to have children in safety and health in the future, or the well-being of herself or close family members if anything is disclosed to police or the authorities.

These spiritual chains have to be addressed and their terror dispersed before women so encumbered can even consider recounting their stories, or finding allies in the prosecuting forces of law enforcement, or the co-operation of the Immigration authorities.

We have learned that, for women who come from religious backgrounds, it is hugely important that they feel spiritually accompanied. It gives them not only comfort, but strength to overcome fear of these curses. There are aspects of loving, Christian ritual which can be hugely supportive.

There are distinct negatives to be addressed among women who come from countries where religion is a powerful cultural force. There are religious teachings which leave women feeling dirty, guilty and deeply ashamed, when the shame of imprisonment and serial rape should truly be laid elsewhere – among her captors and 'clients'.

We know from research undertaken in 'oscillating recovery rates' from various types of trauma that a sense of guilt can inhibit one's ability to move on from trauma. Many of the women with whom we work experience appalling mental torture and harassment during their slavery. They are called names such as 'whore', 'slut', f***** bitch. Their self-esteem is zero when we meet them. And yet, they need good self-esteem and a real awareness of God's love if they are to make a robust recovery and re-enter their own lives with confidence.

So, since guilt and shame are powerful inhibitors to recovery, they need to be dealt with as rapidly as possible. Often, a woman who has been horribly tricked blames herself for her naivety. Since many of her feelings of inadequacy and sin originate in religious constructs, it's important to show her, clearly, that she is in no way to blame for the terrible deceptions and abuses which she has been through.

CHASTE has found that part of building trusting relationships with women who have been trafficked is to be able to manifest God's love in our own lack of condemnation and blame. It is massively important that they begin to feel that the Divine which they have been forced to fear and placate is *already* in action to bring the healing and restoration for which they yearn.

Some find healing in the confessional. Others need to pray and be prayed with. Others need the exchange of religious artefacts and symbols. And some need solely and simply the quiet accepting company of a religious leader or an assigned representative.

These women will need all the spiritual 'building up' that they can get. Many of them will need a very clear sense of God's love before their return to cultures and faith-groups which still see them as 'fallen' women in need of forgiveness, with many ill-disposed to forgive.

We are developing a register of those who are trained and able to offer discrete and reliable accompanying of women who have been trafficked into the United Kingdom.

It is not enough for us to pray *for* these women. We need sensitive, loving, life-giving people who will pray *with* them. If you are interested in helping us in this important support and intervention, please contact our offices.

Jael, the Kenite (Judges 4.15–22)

They wrote songs about me.

They sang them through all the length of Israel. They sang them in Kadesh Barnea when they gathered for the spring lambing. They sang them at Bethel and Shechem when they assembled for the harvest festivals. Drunk or sober, wherever shepherds gathered, they sang about me.

And the women sang too ... in little groups as they waited at the well, or sat by the campfires working the wool, or weaving cloth, using the singing and the song to give rhythm to their work.

Everyone sang songs about me.
Yet none of them knew me at all.

Some might have known Heber, my husband, well enough to greet him on the road, and the womenfolk would have nodded greetings to me as we passed, or spoken if the men were not within earshot. But none of them outside our clan would really have known me at all. And why should they? My story had its pains and grief and flashes of rich delight and moments of a mother's pride, but no more than anyone else's.

When Esther or Reuben died of childhood fevers, I carried on with an ache that has never left me, a void no other child ever fully filled – but that did not make me special. Our people have always found death in the midst of life. Even when my two full-grown sons, Shimri and Joha, were killed in one of the interminable skirmishes with King Jabin's troops (just south of Succoth), I knew that my loss was echoed by the losses of other mothers all across Israel, day in day out, these last twenty years or more.

Even the evening Rebekah never returned from the well and my fears proved worse than true (for someone had reported a sighting of chariots from the King's troop), even then, even through the weeks I nursed her broken and abused body and sought to heal what could not be healed, even when we buried her and her bastard still-born child at her side, my story was not special, it only echoed a hundred mothers' tales all across Israel, while that man Sisera ruled us with his chariots and his armed bully boys in the name of Jabin, King of Canaan.

No, they sang songs about me because of one moment of madness, one moment when all the grief and all the injustice and the hurt of daughters raped, of sons tortured and killed, welled up inside me and drove me on.

You see, he came to me alone and exhausted. It seems his army had been routed and he, Sisera, whose arrogance had crushed our land for twenty years or more, whose chariots had ridden roughshod over us all, whose soldiers had raped and pillaged and killed and enslaved whoever and whenever and wherever they fancied ... this Sisera sought sanctuary in my tent.

Heber and his cousins were gone. They'd taken our remaining flocks to hide in the caves. It was all we had left. They'd gone as soon as news of impending battle reached us. They would not be back for days. I was quite alone, in the tent pitched by the hidden spring close to the summer grazing when he, Sisera, came exhausted, seeking my help.

If he awoke refreshed, who knows what he would have sought to do. But that is not why I did what I did. No. In one instant I thought of all our prayers to Yahweh. My prayers, Heber's prayers, our clan's prayers, twenty years of daily prayers from every household and every tented community and every homeless clan forced to sleep under the stars throughout the length and breadth of the wilderness and the great valley and the mountains.

'Deliver us, O Lord, from the hands of our enemies!'

'Do not turn away from us in our time of need, dear God.'

'Send us one to bring us your justice,
Send us a rescuer to end all our suffering,
Our suffering at the hands of Sisera,
Commander of King Jabin's army.'

A mighty passion seized me, the passion of a whole people's pain, the passion of a God who hurts when we hurt, suffers when we suffer. And with the passion came an anger so vast that it cleared my head and possessed my soul and gave me the strength of ten, the determination of fifty. And so I went searching, searching for something I could use ... anything ... and found both mallet and peg.

In an instant it was done. I know not how, but it was done. There was blood everywhere, yet it was done. Somehow I had driven that great rough-hewn tent peg clear through Sisera's head into the ground beneath. No, truly, in an instant it was done and he was dead. The most feared man in all Israel would never order another raid or burn another house or seize another helpless girl as slave or concubine.

He lay still and twenty years of a people's suffering was ended.

And their singing began.

That is why they sang songs about me all the length of the land. It was that one instant, that one swing of the mallet ...

... and of the rest of my life they knew nothing and they sang nothing.

Yet looking back, it is that one moment that troubles me most. Year after year, in good times and in bad, I did what I could, I cared for my family, I offered thanksgivings to our God, I carried my share of grief without complaint, I treasured my wells of happiness and deep draughts of blessing. My husband Heber knew me and understood; our clan knew me and understood; our God knew me and seemed to understand and that was enough. For me, that was enough.

But in that one moment, what did I do?

Had twenty years of Sisera's violence simply reduced me to his level?

In that instant, did my hand
Become the avenging hand of God?
I do not know, but it troubles me.
And still they sing their songs.

Speaking out

Wherever churches speak, the message should be clear.

Sexual love between humans should be a reflection of Divine Love: self-giving, attentive, generous. Never, *never* for personal gain. It should seek to enhance the life of the Other, never to diminish it.

If the churches can start to explore sexuality on these terms, then we will see an end to the patriarchal attitudes which have turned a very blind eye to male violence against women in the home, on the streets and in our media.

Then we shall see resistance to trafficking for sex; resistance, *again*, to slavery.

Look, the fields of Justice are ripe
Awaiting your harvest,
Spring! Woman
Spring!

From Musa W. Dube 2001. 'John 4:1–42 – The Five Husbands at the Well of Living Waters: The Samaritan Woman and African Women' in Nyambura J. Njoroge and Musa W. Dube (eds), *Talitha cum! Theologies of African Women* **(Pietermaritzburg: Cluster Publications, 2001)**

First

before I weave these words
in prayer and poetry
may burst blood
fall
drop by drop
soak
into the soiled ground
form rivulets
and streams
to reach you
waiting
in the valley

before I compose
this prayer for the poor
and the neglected
and misused
may I answer the doorbell
tend the stranger
an angel unawares

Our responses (John 8.3–11)

The scribes and the Pharisees brought a woman who had been caught in adultery; and made her stand before all of them, and invited Jesus to cast the first stone.

There is an enormous prejudice across the world experienced by women who are caught having sex outside of the marriage bed. Jesus confronts this automatic condemnation *and* the religious leaders who intend to condemn her and stone her to death. The woman stands in front of Jesus, isolated, exposed and (more than likely) naked.

Instead of condemning her Jesus turns the tables. He restores her dignity and turns his male gaze away from her. He asks her accusers for what sin they are accountable to God.

In the world of trafficking and inequalities we are all implicated in the nightmare of trafficking, either as actors or bystanders. We need to see those people who have used trafficked women brought before the judgement of Jesus' gaze – not just those who have pimped, bought and sold, transported raped and beaten.

The male partner is not present in our original story, but today we cannot avoid implicating *all* those who buy and sell her sex.

The woman before Jesus is not condemned. She is brought to a place of safety and understanding. She is given back her future and set on the road to recovery.

This is CHASTE's commitment – to bring women to safety and recovery. And give them back their life.

The cleansing of the temple

The body is a temple,
site of holiness and adoration,
a place of longing and delight,
where intimacy is named as sacred.
But the temple has been desecrated.

Old eyes stare out of a child's face.
Marks of abuse scar a child's flesh.

The temple has become a market-place
where the desperation of poverty
and the longing for a better life
are exploited for profit;
and women's bodies are sacrificed
on the cross of men's lust.

God, see the suffering of your children.

Rise up in anger
and drive out the traders in human flesh
who destroy innocence and abuse trust.

Overturn those
who bring corruption into your courts
and make your temple again
a place of holiness and praise.

A Prayer for Church

Of course we'll get down on our knees.
And say our Thys and say our Thees
And pray amidst the holy gloom
Of our religious sitting-room
Prostrate amongst our polished brasses.
But will we get up off our arses?

Keep looking

Atrocity is hard to look at.

Firstly, the unworthiness and the ugliness of cruelty make us squeamish. We don't wish to become familiar with the detail and the mechanics of excess. We fear contamination. We avert our gaze. (Jesus does not look away. Keep looking.)

Secondly, we feel ourselves helpless and awestruck by really broken, bleeding people. How could you possibly put them back together again? (Well, you can't. But with your help, God can. Keep looking.)

Thirdly we don't want to contemplate such a vast problem. There are so many of these women. How are we as individuals supposed to do anything at all? (You're not. You're going to do it with other people.)

You're having natural reactions. But it's your job not to get stuck with them. Keep looking. If you have any doubt about the existence of sin, here it is pushed right in your face. And you should do something.

Don't fall into the trap of being woolly. Don't get stuck in sixties' liberal, laissez-faire thinking which allows you to convince yourself that sex-slaves (or in fact prostitutes in general) are exercising a 'life-choice' and that no one is being used. If you think this way you're letting yourself off the hook. It is no one's choice to be raped, beaten, tortured and imprisoned.

And don't form the notion that, by association, over time, these women have become contaminated by their treatment. To believe this is to believe that being raped is a sin. You will be in company with a great many other muddled people around the world. Do you want to be?

Keep looking. Each woman's story is different. This is not simple. But don't allow yourself to become comfortably lost in grey areas which prevent you from becoming involved for months, years, a lifetime, while you 'sort out' what you feel about this. How long is a lifetime? Some slaves' lives end up very short.

Keep looking. If you're decent you will. Not with the narrow 'decency' of polite society, which barely contemplates sex, let alone sex-slavery – but the decency which Jesus gave us from the beginning and to which he calls us back in every generation.

The longer we look, the clearer it becomes. To look, properly, at sex-trafficking is to move in the nastiest of worlds, which equals Brady and Hindley in its evil and the Holocaust in its organizational sophistication. In fact, sex-trafficking parallels both of those revolting, human-to-human violations: the weak are completely at the sadistic mercy of the strong. You don't have to look far to see where you stand.

Or do you? If you have any real doubts left about your 'position' in this, remember the many positions sex-trade women will be forced into, on their feet, their stomachs, their backs, their hands and knees, to be raped today.

Then get down on your own knees and thank God that you have not been brought to this. And after you have given thanks, get up and help us.

The old song

I was sixteen, I was beautiful and I was his.
He drove me down avenues of golden pears
And silver nutmeg groves.

An old song blared. We sang along.
I could not but agree;
I wanted to be Bobby's girl,
'The most important thing to me.'

If I'd been Bobby's girl,
If I'd stayed Bobby's girl,
What a thankful, faithful girl I'd be.

We drove through fields of golden rape.
He stopped the car, and beckoned me.
He plumped me down on my thankful knees,
Delighting in my company.

My white dress rubbed to green, green sleeves
While he had me down on that yellow meadow-ground.
As the yellow petals fell all around and around
As the yellow petals fell all around.

Back in the car, an old song blared.
I could not but agree:
'Keep young and beautiful.
It's your duty to be beautiful.'

It's essential to keep beautiful
If you want to be loved.

But a girl who's not a maid
Stays not a girl for long.
He wanted me a green, green girl
But I could not stay so young.
Some younger girl's being driven now
His golden rape among.

Old songs will run in our minds too long.
I cannot but agree.
'Thank heavens for little girls.'
Without them where would little men be?

Alas, my love, you do me wrong
For the sake of your little nut-tree.

'Churches are part of the problem'

Churches are a part of the problem. Most find it impossible to acknowledge the existence of sexual abuse in their own communities and homes, and yet hidden among their members, protected by the culture of silence, they include perpetrators as well as victims of trafficking.

It is not only from the issues of sexual abuse that they shrink. Most have difficulties with sexuality generally.

In a continent whose cultures were shaped within Christian traditions and theologies, among churches whose structures, liturgies and assumptions affirm unequal power relations between women and men, we find ourselves questioning whether the God we worship is really the passionate, creative God who 'created humankind in God's image: in the image of God, God created them male and female God created them'.

We believe that churches have the obligation to provide a counter-cultural impetus in times of political and social change. It is an abuse of bodies, minds and spirits, which are the temple of the Holy Spirit and the dwelling place of the incarnate Christ.

The implications challenge our vision of the Church itself: the household of God in which all have a place and all are honoured.

Profitable business

When asked, the intelligence officers of Operation Pentameter responded that the only correlating factor (across class, ethnicity and nationality) of those profitably engaged in sex-trafficking was that they were usually male.

It's enormously profitable to 'own' slaves. It brings in as much as £120,000 a year for each woman owned.

Sex can be bought in any British town (not just the big cities). New, 'exotic' (that means foreign), compliant (that means frightened), without safety barriers (no condom) sex can be bought for as little as £25 a half-hour.

This should be abhorred by anyone committed to the core values of Christianity. The freedom of one half of humanity to acquire the slave 'services' of sexual labour is not a freedom that can be tolerated any more.

In Sweden legislation has changed, making purchasing sex for money an act of abuse and a violation of women. Clients are now subject to the penalties of the law, in fines and – for persistent offenders – imprisonment. Similar legislation, prosecuting both those who traded and those who purchased, followed the abolition of the slave trade in 1807.

Does the UK still have the courage of its erstwhile anti-slaving convictions?

Sex slavery

Slavery still ambushes and binds
the innocent and the guilty
in a tangling web of lust and cruelty.

In the shadow lands of victim-hood
the gift that God has given is
blunted and tarnished by
body snatchers.

Easy to blame it all on 'them',
but society's connivance in
easy corruption, sating
misdirected desire,
makes us all complicit.

Young lives cower and break
while good people stand by,
and watch,
and do nothing.

© David Grieve

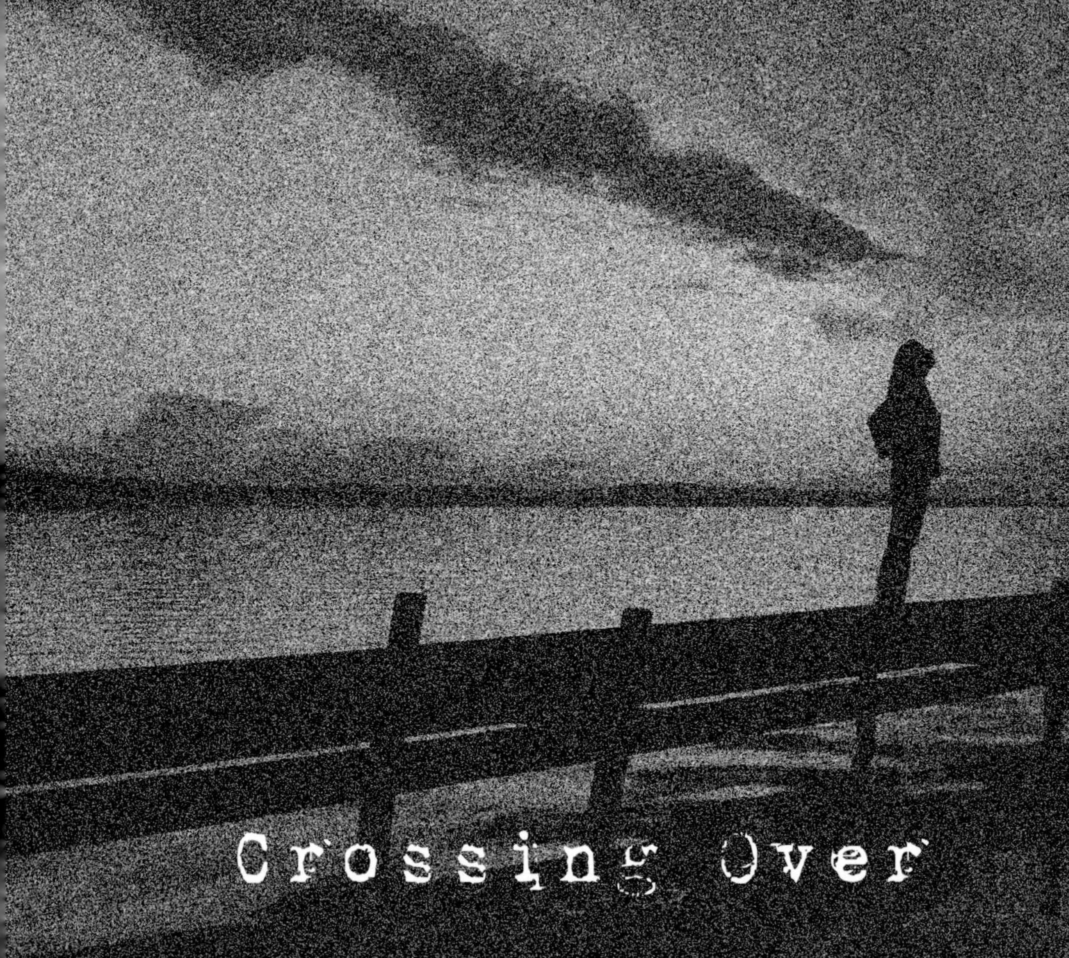

Crossing Over

I am gett'n up and gett'n on, comin home!
And don't want no static bout where I been.
I'm comin HOME an' like the Bible say
'let he who is without sin cast the first stone'.

Sapphire, in *Sex Work: Writings by Women in the Sex Industry*, ed. Frederique Delacoste and Priscilla Alexander (Cleis Press 1998)

Simon the leper: a reflection on Matthew 26.6–13

The room was humming with the easy chat
Of friends content to be together.
I sat apart
Watching him,
Marvelling that he was in my house,
That he counted me a friend.

Then, without warning, I saw her,
Standing on the threshold;
Her presence breaking into conversations,
Which, one by one, fell silent.

She hesitated;
The space around her full of judgements.
I recognized the loneliness, the isolation.
I had known what it felt like, once, before I met him.

And this was her moment for meeting,
For touching.

He looked at her and she stepped forward,
Opening her beautiful jar
And filling the room with its heavy scent.

I could sense the others leaning forward a little,
Disapproving,
Breaths held.
('What would she do next? A woman like her?')

It took courage for her to approach him,
To slowly, gently, pour her perfume over his precious head.
Then she knelt, trembling,
Her head bowed.
And gently, he reached out and raised her face to look into his,
His eyes full of sorrow and tenderness.

'She has done a beautiful thing,' he said.
And I could see from her face, the way she stood and smiled,
that she was no longer alone.

Be myself

Open up the garden through the window of my soul
On the inside it is hollow on the outside it looks whole
Don't know how to change the dry rot that is eating round the frame
Weeds clinging to the cracks all bear the imprint of my name,
Give me time away,
Give me peace, peace to say, yeah:

Lord I find it hard to be myself,
Sometimes when I try I'm just someone else
Though I find it hard, I'm gonna kick back and say,
I wanna be myself today.

Cutting back the hedge rows any hate and bitter years
Weed up all the judgement that compares me with my peers
Step into the field beyond the garden wall
Where there's butterflies and daisies and the grass is growing tall.
It just waves away,
Such a free place to say, yeah:

Lord I find it hard to be myself,
Sometimes when I try I'm just someone else
Though I find it hard, I'm gonna kick back and say,
I wanna be myself today.

You can go and let the black in
Dark clouds that block out all the bright, summer rays, yeah
Just remember they'll be passing,
They're the rain that makes you grow up strong again.

And Lord I find it hard to be myself,
Sometimes when I try I'm just someone else
Though I find it hard, I'm gonna kick back and say,
I wanna be myself today.

Yes though I find it hard I'm gonna kick back and say
I wanna be myself today
I'm gonna be myself today.

Caris: on nurturance

I slipped into life as a woman on the streets without really noticing. I was first put into Care when I was 10 years old. My mother walked out on me before I was 2 – after that I lived with a great aunt and uncle who both died. Then I was with my grandmother who used to beat me. I'd never known my dad and there were no relatives around to take care of me. At the Children's Home I under-achieved at school – and felt nobody really cared for me. There was no nurturance and I suppose I gave myself a ticket to rebel. There weren't any real emotional boundaries put in place for me. It was only later in my 40s I discovered that I'm dyslexic – so no wonder I felt really frustrated and totally under-performed when I was in secondary school.

Anyway, I ended up with no qualifications to talk of. At 16 I met a woman working as a prostitute (although I didn't realize that at the time). She was just arrived in London and had nowhere to sleep, so I took her into my bed-sit where I was staying. We cooked up a great idea to go and live in Sheffield, which never materialized. I went with her to Birmingham where we ran slap-bang into her pimp's brother. She was moved back into working the streets and the pimp took care of *me*.

I was put to work on the streets. I felt absolutely awful, *really* dirty – and I couldn't stop washing myself, trying to wash the dirt away, I guess. I hated it – I would frequently *not* approach any of the cars which were stopping at the street corner I worked. But I had to do some work because if I didn't I had this huge fear of what would happen to me if I came home with no money.

He was really violent. He had grown up on the streets of Kingston, Jamaica, and by the age of 14 was running around carrying guns and keeping out of the way of other gangs – a really violent teenage existence. His parents, who were Christians (he'd been baptized *twice* before he left the Islands), sent him on a one-way ticket to the UK to get him out of the violence which he'd become involved in. He must have got into pimping quite young.

He ran me for seven years. I stayed despite the violence – sometimes I was given such a good hiding I had to play dead in order to survive. Another partner, who was also a pimp, broke my leg. And I still have scars on the back of my head from the beatings and violence which happened then. Sometimes I'd report in at the hospital; they know what's going on but nothing's said. You're just patched up and sent back out again.

I've had two relationships of seven years each with really violent pimps, and carry the scars from those years. They're not just physical scars. They damage you emotionally and relationally for the rest of your life.

People do need to understand that; helping someone recover from this life of abuse is long term and really tough.

You know, I've met him now, a few times, over the last few months. It's been 27 years since I first met him. In a strange way I can understand where he was coming from. I have forgiven him. To meet him and have him say he was sorry for what he did to me then, that has really made a difference to me. I understand now that all the violence, frustration and anger about his life, which had built up in him as a teenager, was worked out on me. He was so violent that he was imprisoned for a while in his 20s.

I never booked him, never went to the police – I did love him and I thought he loved me at the time. When you haven't experienced love (my mother didn't love me, she walked out on me, and my father, as I said, had gone before I was born), then how do you know what love is?

It was only much later when I came to the Lord and I met some Christians who really had compassion and the heart of Christ in them that I discovered what Love was. And that's the story of so many of the others who worked with me on the streets, and in the parlours. No nurturance, no emotional boundaries when young. No Love.

Once you're in that life, you get hardened to it. It's the only way to survive. You start seeing clients as pound signs and that's how it keeps going. Clients are your way of earning a living – after all, you have no other qualifications to do anything else. I'd been on drug and alcohol misuse for many years – that's how you get through.

But as your children grow up – like any mother, you're bothered what your kids think of you. I began to feel dirty again and full of fear that my son was going to find out about what I did ... I wanted desperately to get out but didn't know how to do it. I had no CV – in fact I didn't know what a CV was! No qualifications – no O levels, let alone A levels. When I went along to the Job Centre, they asked me what I had been doing for the last 28 years of my life. What was I supposed to say? I'd been a lady of leisure? I don't think so!

Getting *out* of prostitution is the toughest thing. I remember we used to sit around in the kitchen and the sitting-room of the brothels we worked, and talk about how we were all going to be getting out of this life in the next few months or next year. When we had earned enough to get free – to raise some rent, get some qualifications. We all sang the same song. But we were all in bondage really – just we didn't realize it.

None of us had any qualifications, no way of talking to society – except through selling sex. And that doesn't fit into the way society outside the parlour works. We had no skills. We didn't know how to engage – we were stuck. The ones who remained behind are still stuck. Most of them really want to get out. That's what we used to talk about between clients. But they don't know how to. The support needed to get out is enormous.

I've been on a real learning curve. I had no qualifications, nothing, from my years in education, at the Children's Home, years of putting up with violence, name-calling and abuse. My strongest support and friendships were with women who were working with me. It's the toughest thing breaking free, making that long journey to cross over. You have to put all the trappings that go along with that life behind you and walk away from everything that helped you through the day – the drugs, the alcohol, the chat and support of the other women.

Drugs are really significant in the working pattern of the parlours. They help you get through long working days, they keep you trim. If you keep your figure you've got more chance of being picked by clients when we all line up like cattle for collection. I have worked dozens of parlours and been with thousands of clients. You lose count. The drugs and the alcohol help numb your emotions so that you can get through the ordeal. Most of my life in prostitution, on the streets or in the parlours, has been an ordeal. What you keep thinking is: 'How do I get out and what do I do the other side of all this? What has happened to my life from 16 to 44? What have I got to show for it?'

In the main, I feel the clients were a nightmare. Some of them, of course, were just sad people. They weren't really coming for the sex, just wanted someone to listen to them and give them a bit of attention. Those ones, I know it sounds daft, but for those I felt some compassion. But for the most part it was just for the sex. But you grow in discernment. The longer you work in this world the better you get at communication. You learn how to listen and to talk in a way which really limits the time you have to endure, so the sex bit doesn't last long. Then you don't have to put up with being humped for half an hour at a time.

In the end what really made me leave was that I couldn't stand being touched, groped and humped any longer. It got to the stage where I said, 'I want my body back!' I couldn't keep taking people's money and not give them any goods back in return.

I'm so glad that I'm the other side of it now. Lots of my friends are still working. They haven't been able to get out. They haven't had the level of support that's vital to be able to get out. They have no formal education, no access to the help required, no purpose. No skills are being made available to them, which are essential to start making contact, making connection with a life the other side of prostitution.

You need your emotional self-esteem rebuilt. It's on the floor when you come out of prostitution. People want to know: *Where have you been? What have you been doing?* What can you say? You need an awful lot of support. It needs something really structured at local council level, all over the country, to deal with the women who are trying to break free.

The route I was fortunate enough to take was through the Church – real tangible practical love. First I had to survive five years of the religious sort of response – being prayed for, blessed and then, basically, being told to 'get on with it'. But recently I've had a much more practical church life, with people really bothered to help, do the practical stuff of helping me get a CV together, talk around what is needed to get a job, help me through the tough times; sometimes it feels it would be easier to go back rather than continue trying to get out.

You need purpose – a real purpose if you're going to get out. And real, practical, loving support. Without that you can have hope and faith that things can be different, but without a purpose which can be *realized*, you think 'why bother?' It is *so* tough. You need nurturance, affirmation and purpose. These are the three big things that need to come towards a woman trying to exit – and it is so hard. *So* very hard.

Caris (not this woman's real name), © CHASTE

Where there is love

Where there is love,
Desire is holy.

Where there is love,
Laughter heals.

In your gaze I find peace.

By your touch
I learn who I am.

I face risk and conquer fear
Where there is love.

'I am a strong and competent person and have much to offer'

I had an unhappy childhood. My mum was abusive towards me and all my brothers and sisters. In early teenage I kept running away from home. No one ever asked why. I was just a bad kid. I had a social worker but she was useless; she just believed everything my mum told her. She was never there for me.

At 14 I ran away one more time. But on that occasion I met someone. He was a lot older than me but he was kind and soon said how much he loved me. At first he took me to a friend of his; he said if I would look after her children while she went out to work, I could live there for free. I thought the work was strange, as she went out at all different times and not for very long but seemed to come back with plenty of money.

After a while he suggested that I moved in with him and told me how I could earn a lot of money. So I started to work on the streets. It was scary standing on street corners. But I soon earned enough to pay all the bills for the flat; I was paying for everything for my 'boyfriend'. He took nearly all the money from me. If I came home with no money, I was battered. Badly battered. The only 'excuse' that he found acceptable was if I produced a bail-note to say I'd been arrested for being a 'common prostitute'.

That's another point. Over all those years I was fined £5,860 for 'working'. What was the point of that? How was I expected to pay the fines without going out on the street to work again? Why did no one ever suggest another way forward?

I put up with this for about four years. Once I saved up over £1000 and bought a TV and a video. Then the final straw came when I was 17. He sold them both for £250 in order to buy his drugs. I had had enough.

So one day, early in the morning, I ordered a removal van and moved everything out of the flat. I found a new flat and started working for myself. I earned good money, furnished my flat well and had plenty of nice clothes. But in the end, money wasn't enough. Prostitution is the loneliest job in the world. You have no friends outside the world of other working women. You are completely cut off from the rest of society. A few women, like me, manage to keep their own money and earn plenty of it. But it's not worth it. You need something that earns you self-respect as well. And, more importantly, any respect from other people.

Eventually I met a wonderful woman from the Maze Marigold project. For the first time in my life I experienced unconditional love. It was amazing; she was amazing. She won not only my trust but the trust of plenty of other working women – and that's a considerable achievement.

So I have stopped working. It hasn't been an easy journey. All too often I'm barred from employment – sometimes even educational courses – because of my criminal convictions. I'm told I'll have to wait five years for them to become no longer relevant. I can't wait five years. But I *am* now a qualified trainer and am determined to continue to find work where my experience can really be used and also my skills be developed – and I can be respected and wanted for who I am and what I can do in my own right. I am a strong and competent person and have much to offer.

So much more needs to be *done* in our society to prevent my experiences continuing to be those of many, many other women. There is now much talk about the scandal of international sex-trafficking. What about all the trafficking of girls and young women being sent round *this* country from city to city to make money for their pimps?

Why are the women still criminalized while so little effort is made to arrest their pimps? They drive round in their posh cars, supposedly on Income Support. So much other crime would also be stopped if attention were directed to them.

I See You

I see the new You,
The way you've always been.
I see you standing tall and strong,
Confident and clean.

I see the true You,
The way you really are.
I see
Beyond the things you see.
I see you free.

No matter what's been said to you,
No matter what's been done,
No matter what's been put on you,
My will for you will still be done.

I see the new You,
The way you've always been.
I see you standing tall and strong,
Confident and clean.

I see the true You,
The way you really are.
I see beyond the things you see.
I see you free.

I see
Beyond the things you see,
I see you free.

Exchanged for a second-hand car

Saadia (not her real name) is from India. In 2004 she was persuaded to take a job in the UK, working as a model. The job offer was bogus. When she arrived here her passport was taken. She was kept in a house with other women and forced to work in a dancing club. She was threatened with violence by her captors. They told her that her family back home would be killed if she didn't comply. She was sold on from that club to another club. She was forced to have sex with clients. She was sold on a number of times in this way. Eventually she was sold for a second-hand car.

Saadia managed to escape and, through a church minister, she was able to contact CHASTE. By building up trust with Saadia over a number of weeks her story started to unfold. It was possible to put her in touch with agencies in this country who could investigate her information. Measures were taken against her captors. Most importantly we were able to place Saadia in a safe-house where she could be looked after and where she could begin the long road to healing.

Safe-house

I have been made dirty
From the inside out.
So much,
So very much dirt
Pushed inside me.

In this clean room
I am the only dirty thing.
Can you get clean
From the outside in?

Tribute to Saa

Saa was a prostitute in Bangkok. A few months ago she died. She was 27. She didn't die because she had contacted HIV/AIDS or some other sexually transmitted disease. She didn't die because of the countless beatings in the brothel or because of violent abuse. She didn't die as a result of the several abortions she'd undergone. She died because she was poor and poverty has few choices.

Saa died because of a physical condition, encephalitis (or 'water on the brain') which, had she been born to a wealthier family, could have been treated. At the time of her birth, doctors would have discovered her condition. She would have received medical help.

But Saa was born into a very poor family in north-east Thailand. She had only primary schooling, as village girls commonly do. Her parents were rice farmers with only a small piece of land - just enough to produce rice for the family, but little to sell. The rising charges of the middlemen leave little or no profit for rice-growers. Tradition dictates that it is the duty of elder daughters to go to the city to find work to support the family. In most families this is not a choice.

So, when she was 16 years old, Saa came to Bangkok. She had scant education and no work skills. Her choices were limited; she could work in a construction gang for small reward. With a little capital she could run a market stall, or cook food and sell it in the market. But she had no capital.

To enable her to make the money that her family needed, Saa's only 'choice' was prostitution. Working as a dancer in a bar and 'going with customers' would provide the amount needed to support her family. The demand of sex-tourists, foreign residents and local men means there is always plenty of work in Bangkok. So Saa began working as a prostitute in a bar in Patpong Road, the city's largest, most notorious red-light district. First she was a waitress, then as a go-go dancer Saa began her life in prostitution.

Years passed. Saa worked in several bars. She had hundreds of clients, one son and three abortions. She didn't know much about birth control and, anyway, couldn't afford it. If a client refused to use a condom she had no choice. Neither could she choose her clients, working in the bar as she did.

One day, Saa chanced to visit the Rahab Beauty Shop in Patpong Road (a Christian outreach ministry to women in prostitution), to have her hair and make-up done. One of the Thai staff told her about the love of Jesus Christ; how he could give her new life and the peace that she had sought for so long. Saa cried and said: *If only I had come to Rahab and known about this before I wouldn't have had so much pain and suffering!*

The following day Saa left the bar and came to work at Rahab Bazaar, an income-generation project. She responded to the gospel and began attending a local church regularly. She became involved with their programme caring for disabled orphan children. A few months later she fulfilled a long-time dream: she began studying to be a hairdresser.

Saa worked as a hairdresser at Rahab Ministries for three years. People commented on her radiant smile, her joy, her obvious love for God and the beauty of God in her life. Her one desire was to serve Jesus whom she loved so much. Then God took Saa for himself, to plant her, a beautiful flower, in his garden.

Saa's life wasn't wasted after all. She brought joy and hope into our lives at Rahab. She gave me joy. Today she is in a better place. But I know that Saa's death was hastened by lack of choice, which is the huge price of poverty.

Reaching Safety

It was the Lord himself who brought us and our fathers up out of the land of slavery. He protected us on our entire journey and among all the nations through which we travelled.

Joshua 24.17

Safe as houses

For most of us personal safety is something that we take for granted. We may find our work stressful, or the journey to work exhausting, but we carry with us the belief that if we decide to do the normal things of life (such as going shopping, visiting the dentist, or talking to family and friends) it will happen.

However, for some people the perception that the world is a safe and predictable place where they can move freely, taking advantage of simple pleasures in life, is totally absent. Victims of human-trafficking (particularly those involved in sex-trafficking) find that nothing is predictable and that the world is a painful and dangerous place. For many of the women who have managed to escape from this slavery, the concept of a safe, secure home does not exist.

Yet the creation of safe-houses is absolutely essential: in the midst of their distress, disorientation and trauma (caused by multiple rape, enforced substance-abuse, physical violence), they can begin to rediscover what it means to be human.

To those who have never experienced what it is like to be deprived of our personal and emotional freedom, it may be difficult to understand why young women would allow themselves to be put in such difficult and distressing situations.

Why don't they just walk away from their pimps and traffickers? The problem is that their physical, emotional and spiritual deprivation is of such a magnitude that they become totally compliant, in the misguided belief that this will reduce their level of abuse and trauma.

So what can we do? It is vital that safe-houses are set up and maintained to provide the supportive, caring environments where the many, many needs of these exhausted and frightened women can be met by caring people experienced (and suited) to working with such a vulnerable group.

For staff working in safe-houses, adequate training and support are essential. This is not work for the fainthearted. But for people who have a calling to this kind of work it can be extremely rewarding.

While religion and spirituality may not be for everyone, it is my experience that the practice of mindfulness and prayer is an important means of making sense of what often does not appear to make any sense.

Just as our safe-houses need strong foundations, it is important that we who are involved in these highly demanding caring roles are aware and responsive to our own needs for solid beliefs and values to support our practice.

The round table

I sat round the table in Autumn 2004 with nine other women representatives from various church denominations. I was carrying in my mind and heart the seven women whom I'd met who had been trafficked for sex and then returned to their countries of origin – because there was 'no room at the Inn'.

Having worked in Immigration control as a Religious Manager I knew the Government was funding the Poppy Project with 27 fully funded beds for survivors. I also knew that this was an under-resourced response to a huge need; so many women out there in our cities, suburbs, brothels, secured-houses.

'We could do something from the resources of the churches we represent,' I said.

Helen from the Salvation Army agreed. So did Sister Ann from the Conference of Religious. Rising from her chair, her face flushed with emotion: 'We should do something – we've got to do *something*.'

All agreed. We prayed that God would show us what to do next and who to ask. We prayed for the resilience and faith we would need to match the Government's provision.

Little more than two years later, at the end of January 2007, out of the energies and vision gathered around that round table,18 more fully funded bed spaces are available across Britain. They are funded by the Salvation Army and the Medaille Trust, tapping into the resources of religious congregations up and down the country.

Meanwhile CHASTE is progressing further resourcing in step-forward housing with an independent housing provider developing apartments, where women who are recovering from the physical and emotional trauma of being trafficked can feel their way into more independent living – and begin to make plans for long-term employment.

CHASTE's *time for a®rest campaign* (launched at a large Christian youth festival, Soul Survivor, in the summer of 2006) had thousands of cards pouring into the Home Office, to MPs' and Ministers' offices. We called for the immediate signing of the Council of Europe's Convention on Action Against Trafficking in Human Beings. This provides for appropriate recovery time for victims of trafficking, with full medical, psychological, legal and welfare needs being met from the state purse.

People signed online from the CHASTE website and added their electronic voices to tens of thousands of cards which poured in from women's groups, youth meetings and individual church members into Westminster, urging the Government to sign up to the proper care of vulnerable and abused women. In March 2007, the Government signed.

Safety for ex-trafficked women is an absolute prerequisite, if they are to get permanently out of the clutches of their pimps and traffickers. Safe, discrete and supported safe-housing must be available. It is simply not an option to place women in B&Bs – or worse, into Immigration Detention and Removal Centres. They either disappear or despair. Some even get prostituted again from B+Bs.

That CHASTE round-table meeting represents a step-change in the provision of safe-housing options in the United Kingdom.

All the costs have been covered until the middle of 2009 by the denominations who have undertaken this intervention. However, it is simply not sustainable or appropriate for the churches to continue, out of their limited budgets, to underwrite what our country's government should be undertaking on a far, far greater scale. Especially since, Britain needs to be showing itself sensitive to the abuse which its own citizens have heaped on innocent foreign women.

CHASTE wishes to see the Government providing, from the Exchequer, adequate funds to pay the recovery needs of all those whom the Police and Immigration Authorities discover each year to have been trafficked for sex into the UK.

It would be a drop in the ocean for the Government: less than the cost of a second-class stamp, per tax-paying adult. It would be a warning to traffickers across the world, and a letter of hope to those they exploit, that enough is enough.

Freedom

Like a deer longing for water, Freedom, you are far.
How long should I wait to be with you Freedom?
Night may embrace me and moon smile down upon me
But I am perceived as a black sheep out in the left field.
In schools, hospitals and police stations you are nowhere to be seen;
I am dog-tired of looking for you, Freedom.

To express myself is forbidden;
I am still frightened to further get hold of you.
From Cape to Cairo, Freedom you are not fully fledged.
My heart locks on you but my fellows ignore you.
When will you free me from this bondage?

Drowning or dreaming

On the crossroads, my mind becomes circumspect.
Even the air looked worried at my insane behaviour.

Why run away from the lion's den and seek cheetah's help?

Deep in the vibrating valley, I looked like a lost calf.
Comfort and sympathy never crossed my path.

My plea for the sanctuary put me behind bars.
Drowning or dreaming, I was out of my mind.
Tears streaming my face, I was an injured kitten.
Refuge was denied.
Sanctuary was denied.

The lion I fled begins to haunt me.
My head recalls the horrific pictures.

I lay dumb like rocks
In limbo
Awaiting disaster to engulf me.

Psalm for safety

Oh God, your breath is my life.
I call down your spirit to protect me.
Breathe over me and into me,
Save me from death, danger and despair.

Oh God, your breath is fire,
Your hands are made of fire.

You hold me:
I am cupped in your hands,
Held like a child.

Fire within,
Fire without,
No one can get through.

I breathe in your power.

Your fire keeps me hidden
And my heart is safe.

© Christina Rees

Freedom

Free from the hurt
Free from the pain
Free from the neighbours pointing fingers again.

Free from the fear of losing her for ever.
Free from the tears.
Free from the strain.
Free from the fear of her missing again.

Free to sleep.
Free to laugh.
Free to sing and dance in the rain.
Free to go out and come back home again.

Free to eat.
Free from self-harm.
Free to enjoy peace and calm.

Free from the hurt.
Free from the pain.
Free to live life to the full again.

© CROP

Prayer of the brothel girl (John 4.7–26)

If I could reach the outside
I would go to a bar.
A nice, ordinary bar.
The ordinariness of the bar
Would be heaven to me.

If I could reach the outside,
Waiting in the bar, for his friends,
Some man might talk to me,
Asking, truly, no more,
Nothing more of me
Than a drink.

And I would fetch him his drink.
And he would say;
'You thirst for more than
Ordinary drink, I think.'
'So true!' I'd frown.
And what he'd tell me next
Would almost knock me down.

He'd tell me everything I'd ever done,
Everything I'd had done,
So many times, to me.
Passing before me;
One finished, forgive-able movie.

I would just be a girl
Who had got wrong and then
Been reached on my right side
To begin again;

If I could reach the outside.

A place of hope and possibilities

Reflecting back over the past six months I marvel at all that has happened in my life!

On 2 October 2006 I began work with the Medaille Trust as Manager of one of their safe-houses. My previous job, as a youth worker, had been directing a retreat centre for young people.

It all seems like a long time ago! I remember, on that first day, sitting down in the house (which had been donated by a group of religious sisters), and thinking to myself '*Now* what do I do?'

I had only just moved into the area myself – I didn't know the area or a single person in it. In those very early days, I didn't want to introduce myself to anyone in case they asked me what my job was; I was hyper-careful over revealing anything about the house.

I knew I needed to begin with some very basic jobs, like changing the phone number to one that couldn't be traced. But that's not as simple as it sounds! It took me six full days to remedy – don't ask.

Getting a PO Box number, to keep our actual address secret, is virtually impossible. It's taken us until now to work out that PO Box addresses are not 100 per cent safe.

Have you tried registering with a GP recently? You need bills and things to prove that you live in the Borough. *Not* things that traumatized, dispossessed, foreign nationals can provide. As I write I can still feel the frustration of those early days rising up within me.

Since then we've employed a full quota of staff. I can't tell you how happy I was as I saw the team building up; a team of fine, dedicated, skilled women. Although at the same time, I was terrified that, since I was learning at the same time as they were, I might not (in fact did not) have the answers all to their questions.

From 8 January we had an intense induction, lasting three full weeks, exploring as many different issues as we could. This was really important and empowered us, as a team, to move forward. But nothing really prepared us for the reality of working with women survivors of sex-trafficking.

Part of my role is to liaise with many, many other organisations. This involves attending many meetings. During my first CHASTE round-table meeting of housing providers I wanted the ground to come and swallow me up. Everyone seemed to know everything! They seemed to be talking in a different language.

It was then that I almost handed in my resignation – a feeling of total inadequacy engulfed me. How on earth could I be adequately qualified to carry out this role? How could I learn enough to work alongside the police, the health service, Immigration, social services, housing, etc., etc., etc.?

The answer came to me, '*I won't*'. And once I realized this, the job seemed far less daunting. As a staff we all pull together and work well together. We pool our knowledge, resources and strengths. Outside of our own little house there's the St John of God Service which offers so much guidance and support. Moving out further there are so many organisations, such as CHASTE, that have been towers of strength for us – we're not alone.

On 3 March 2006, we welcomed the first woman into our house. We were delighted that after five weeks of research and policy-setting and anticipation and waiting we were about to begin 'the real work'.

There was a feeling of all being in it together, a wonderful atmosphere of hope and celebration that something was happening for women who had been treated so terribly. And that we are involved in one of the most topical issues that there is in our society right now.

Since then we have been on a very steep learning curve and the women who stay with us here have taught us so much.

So, I journey on – in the knowledge that we are doing our best. Sometimes my heart is full of hope and at other times filled with sadness. We can't make everything better but our little house is a place of hope and possibilities.

Liturgy, Prayers and Hymns

To clasp one's hands in prayer is the beginning of an uprising against the disorder of the world.

Karl Barth

When our hearts are wintry

When our hearts are wintry
and Death's savagery still
attacks and cheats us of the
joys we were meant to embrace,

Lord, draw near and walk beside us,
risen, conquering Son.

When the soil of our sorrow is
hard to break and ice surrounds
our souls, keeping them numb,

Lord, draw near and walk beside us,
risen, conquering Son.

When our future looks black and senseless,
and we don't know how to begin again,
because light has fled from our lives,

Lord, draw near and walk beside us,
risen, conquering Son.

Meet us, greet us,
take us by the hand and
pull us to our feet
so that we may walk with you
in the way that leads to eternal life.

The love of God

What can separate us from the love of God?
Can seething anger at the ugly violence against women?
No nothing can separate us from the love of God.

Can the weeping of mothers for daughters sold into slavery?
No nothing can separate us from the love of God.

Can acquired immune deficiency?
No nothing can separate us from the love of God.

Can despair over the dread disease?
No nothing can separate us from the love of God.

Can hatred and rejection?
No nothing can separate us from the love of God.

Can politicking and panic?
No nothing can separate us from the love of God.

Can the fear of dying?
No nothing can separate us from the love of God.

Can the cries of infants infected at birth?
No nothing can separate us from the love of God.

Can the wailing of orphans?
No nothing can separate us from the love of God.

You are God

You are the Shelter in the raging storms
You are the Hope when there is no hope
You are the Saviour in the midst of suffering
You are the embracing Arms in the darkest night
You are the Door that is never shut
You are the Love of the loveless
You are the Light in the darkness of death
You are the Candle lit for the loved one
You are the Nurse nurturing the diseased
You are the HIV-positive body carrying the stigma
You are the dying One consoling the bereft
You are the suffering Friend to the end.

© Deverakshanam Betty Govinden

Blanket and pillow – a blessing

May the roots of faith grow strong within you.
May your vision of peace be like a clear sky.
May you be touched by the lightning flash of bright hope.
May you drink deeply at the well of joy.
May the love of God
Be your blanket and your pillow,
Your bed and your room,
And may God's arms surround you
Now and forever more.
Amen.

© Christina Rees

Sometimes (Job 23.1–9, 16–17)

Suggested tune: You shall go out with joy

Sometimes we want a fight,
a chance to put You right,
to explain how what You've done feels cruel and heartless;
then we long to show
we're the people who know
how You should play Your part.

Chorus:
Gracious God, at such times
we need You there,
whether seen or unseen,
please prove You care.
Take our hurt and our rage and blank despair
and hold us with Your love.

Sometimes we stand and stare,
as if no God was there,
and our prayers would die away with no one to hear them.
Then our hopes subside
we feel empty inside –
alone with hurt and fear.

Sometimes we turn and run
and wish the end would come,
as we simply cannot take the pain that's around us
then we long to be
from existence set free –
be lost and never found.

Confession

Almighty God, our creator and healer, you know our journeys
The places where we fall, the bruises we carry,
The fractures we sustain in ignorance, perversity or weakness.
We bring you our lives and the World's life – and ask for healing.
Forgive our feeble indifference, our avoidance of abandoned souls.
While we celebrate, women and children are
Prostituted, attacked, enslaved.
Forgive our delight in committees and delay.
Bring healing and restoration to us.
Open our blinded eyes, strengthen our weary limbs.
In Christ's name, Amen.

Confession

Almighty God, our creator and healer,
who knows our hearts and minds,
there are things that are wrong
with ourselves and the world.

We are blind in chosen ignorance
and we are blind as we turn deliberately away.
Forgive our feeble excuses for indifference
to the evil enslavement of women
and our acceptance of a culture that makes trafficking possible.
Forgive our pettiness of church
that seeps away our energy into
trivia, defensiveness and nonsense.

All this we repent
in the sure knowledge that your forgiveness
will bring us to action.
Amen.

Absolution

God of encircling peace,
God of restoration,
God who causes Justice to pour down and drench us with Mercy,
deliver, pardon and rescue you,
support you into wholeness
and bring us all into the healing of God's Kingdom.

© Carrie Pemberton

Divine power – a blessing

Love is Divine Power.
Divine Power is Love.

May the power of divine love
Fill you, protect you and give you peace,
Now and always.
Amen.

© Christina Rees

Franciscan prayer for an end to trafficking

Lord of freedom and love,
we are saddened to know that
more than one million people
are trafficked into slavery each year.

The effects of contemporary slavery
are felt in every country where we work.

As sons and daughters of our Father,
we are tormented by this reality
which leaves devastating repercussions for generations to come.

Our hearts grieve for what our minds can barely comprehend,
particularly when we hear of women, men and children
deceived and transported to unknown places.

We recognize that this sexual and economic exploitation occurs
because of human greed and profit.
We are sorrowful and our spirits angry
that human dignity is being degraded
through deception and threats of force.

Help the violators to be transformed and enlightened;
to realize the scope of their unjust actions.

Allow them to see the value and the dignity
of every human person.

As religious who serve the poor in a spirit of peace and justice,
we must protest this atrocity and work
against the demeaning practice of human trafficking.

Lord of Life,
strengthen those whose hearts have been broken
and whose lives have been uprooted.

Give us the light, grace and courage to work
with you so that we can all participate in the goodness of creation.
Fill us with the wisdom and courage to stand
in solidarity with the victims
so that we may all enjoy the freedoms and rights
which have their source
in your Son and our Lord Jesus Christ.

Eucharistic prayer

The Lord has called our name.
His Spirit is with us.

Lift up your hearts!
We lift them to the Lord!

Gentle and creative Word,
the desire of our heart.
We come to your table to seek your grace,
to offer our thanks and praise,
because loving us, before we understood love,
you became bruised for us.

Forgiving our weakness
your kingship breaks into the world
so that on Easter morning
we know the touch of the anointed one
and we are named resurrection people.

Therefore with Mary, who knelt at your feet
and broke open her precious perfume
to anoint you as messiah,
with all who seek you,
with those who weep costly tears,
who stretch their hand to anoint the broken,
who come to your table for healing,
and find that they are remembered ...
with all your saints,
who made themselves vulnerable,
we praise you saying:

Holy, holy, holy Lord,
God of welcome and touch,
Heaven and earth are full of your glory.
Hosanna in the highest.
Blessed is the one who comes in the name of the Lord.
Hosanna in the highest.

Blessed is Jesus Christ, our Lord
Who let himself be found
and bids us welcome to his table
Who saves us with freely offered forgiveness
and accepts those rejected by the world.

Amen. Lord, call us by name,
that we may announce
that you have broken the power of sin.

Jesus offered his love for sinners,
opening wide his arms on the cross.
He set us free to be anointed with him,
to proclaim that our weeping will end.

Amen. Lord, call us by name,
that we may announce
that you have broken death!

On the night that he offered himself
he sat at table with his friends
took bread, gave thanks, broke it, and said
'This is my body, which is for you.
Do this to remember me.'
In the same way also the cup, after supper, saying:
'This cup is the new covenant made in my blood.
Do this, as often as you drink it, in remembrance of me.'

Amen. Lord, call us by name,
that we may announce
you as messiah!

So we remember all that Jesus did for Mary.
We proclaim your new fellowship
that by your sacrifice and forgiveness you have saved us
and that we too are called to announce new beginnings.

Come then Holy Spirit
pour out your priceless oil of gladness and love
on us and our gifts of bread and wine,
that we too may recognize the face of the Lord.

Amen. Come Holy Spirit.

The service continues with the Lord's Prayer.

Magnificat (Luke 1.46–55)

To the tune of 'Barbara Allen'

My soul doth magnify my God.
My spirit hails my saviour!
For you have not looked down on me,
My tribe or my behaviour.

Behold, henceforth I am raised up
And folk will bid me blessing,
New generation upon old
As God's will is progressing.

Great things, Almighty, you have done
To me your maid and maiden.
Your name is holy as the trust
With which I now am laden.

Your mercy and forgiveness fall
On those who love and fear you,
Across the many centuries
For all who would be near you.

You scatter wide the narrow ones
Whose hearts' imagination
Has grown too haughty and too proud
Among your own creation.

Unseating those with power and might
You put them in their places.
You starve out greediness and sin
And feed the tragic faces.

You helped your servants find their way;
The father and the mother
And, unborn, yet, the seeds of God
As sister and as brother.

Adapted by Lucy Berry for CHASTE

Hymn: a sharpened tent peg (Judges 4–5)

Suggested tune: Aberystwyth

Did oppression, year on year;
rape and pillage, hurt and fear;
callous violence for the state
earn this man his pointed fate?

Can we share the seer's delight –
Debra's joy at wrong put right,
or must we resist her song –
say this tent peg, too, is wrong?

Watch as Jael, a nomad's wife;
poor, oppressed through all her life;
in this moment, roles reversed,
kills the killer, unrehearsed.

Yet we also see the pain
as a mother waits in vain;
kept by violence, harsh and long,
is she right or is she wrong?

Now the story's pointed peg
presses hard against our head:
who is wrong and who is right
where is darkness, where God's light?

Learning his love: a response to Galatians 3.28

Suggested tune: Let There Be Love

If Christ has made no distinction,
died for us all on the cross,
if we are all truly special,
all worth his pain and his loss,
then we must each learn to value
those we'd despise or ignore;
risk being changed by this challenge –
learning his love.

If Christ adopts Jews and Gentiles,
welcomes the whole human race,
finds deep delight in the beauty
of each unique human face,
then we must each dare to welcome
strangers we once might have feared
risk being changed by this challenge –
learning his love.

If Christ rejects stark injustice
where some are slaves, some are free,
died to release ev'ry captive,
so they may be who they'll be,
then we must each fight for fairness
cease to enslave or exploit,
risk being changed by this challenge –
learning his love.

If Christ includes men and women,
valuing each as they are,
that they may all be respected,
find their esteem on a par,
then we must all work to alter
what our forefathers assumed,
risk being changed by this challenge –
learning his love.

Lost in traffick – chaplain's prayer

Long journey into story:
lost in traffick,
meeting by Night's light
language of signs and wonders
bed of safety, bed of delight.

Stories peeling from skin.
Life in scabs and broken bones.
Sweat and semen-stained tears
bringing prayer; struggling to fight
the shock of the untold Godliness.

God give me grace to be.
God save me from temper –
and the safety of not caring.

But above all, God,
let there be no more stories
and journeys into the night.

For I have heard enough
and your daughters are dying.

In the name of your son who hears stories ...

Vicious tales (Genesis 16 and 21; Judges 19; Exodus)

Suggested tune: Glorious Things of Thee are Spoken

Vicious tales of slaves and masters
Scattered through the Bible show
After three long, wrong millennia
We are changing very slow.
Hagar: slave-girl who bore Ishmael
First-born son of Abraham,
Left to starve and hear her baby
Crying, dying in the sand.

Or the nameless girl, whose savaged
Limbs were severed joint from joint,
Parcelled up and sent through Judah,
While her master proved his point.
Such dark depths of desolation,
Loneliness to make you wince,
Humans terrorizing humans
Happened every century since.

Nothing equals or surpasses
Israel under Egypt's lash –
Except Africa abducted
Ravished, sold for ready cash.
Except slave-girls in our cities'
Cellars, attics, box-room jails
Groomed and kidnapped, raped, assaulted.
God! How like the bible tales.

Scattered concubines and daughters;
Lord! our memory is short
If we truly have forgotten
How our liberty was bought.
Scattered concubines, our daughters,
Parcelled, shipped to Amsterdam,
Acton, Airdrie, Aberystwyth.
Are we Christ – or Abraham?

March of the women

Shout, shout, up with your song!
Cry with the wind, for the dawn is breaking;
March, march, swing you a-long,
Wide blows our banner, and hope is waking.
Song with its story, dreams with their glory
Lo! They call, and glad is their word!
Loud and louder it swells,
Thunder of freedom, the voice of the Lord!

Long, long – we in the past
Cowered in dread from the light of heaven,
Strong, strong – stand we at last,
Fearless in faith and with sight new given.
Strength with its beauty, Life with its duty
(Hear the voice, oh hear and obey!)
These, these – beckon us on!
Open your eyes to the blaze of day.

Comrades – ye who have dared
First in the battle to strive and sorrow!
Scorned, spurned – nought have ye cared,
Raising your eyes to a wider morrow,
Ways that are weary, days that are dreary,
Toil and pain by faith ye have borne;
Hail, hail – victors ye stand,
Wearing the wreath that the brave have worn!

Life, strife – those two are one,
Naught can ye win but by faith and daring.
On, on – that ye have done
But for the work of today preparing.
Firm in reliance, laugh a defiance
(Laugh in hope, for sure is the end)
March, march – many as one,
Shoulder to shoulder and friend to friend.

Ethel Smythe, Suffragette (1858–1944)

Another's freedom to hurt me: antiphonal prayer

Based on Psalm 119.134: 'Redeem me from the oppression of men.'

Compassionate God,
No one hears my voice.

No one comes near to me.
No one sees my shame.

Where is my neighbour?
Where is my friend?
Where is my companion?

I am abused, rejected, beaten, dirty and afraid.
I am ignored and forgotten like a statistic to the world.
Is this life for me?

Is this what you created me to be:
A slave imprisoned by another's freedom to hurt me?

My body is broken and scarred.
My mind is battered by hate.

The feeling in my heart is like stone, numb to the pain.
My legs are bruised and my eyes filled with a bitter saltiness.
My breath is all but lost.

I am abandoned.

No one hears my voice.
No one comes near to me.
No one sees my shame.
Where is my neighbour?
Where is my friend?
Where is my companion?

I am far away from home, far away from joy,
Far away from play and far away from comfort

Am I far from you, God?

Are you here with me, God?
Are you crushed like me?
Are you also despised and rejected?
Are you also oppressed and afflicted?

Are you with me, abandoned,
And cut off by the world?

I cry out, but it is like a whisper in the ocean.
Are you silenced like me?

Come, Compassionate God.
Come and sit with me and listen to me.

Come and help me, once again, to stand.
Come and walk with me and help me,
Once again, to be considered equal.

Come and free me that I may be human again.
Come and heal me from this wrath of man.

Open my eyes, God! I want to see you.

May I see you, God,
In the face of someone who rescues me in your name?

A morning salutation

Suggested tune: Golden Slumbers

Morning Sun breaks and fills the skies.
God's own dear Love will still surprise.
As in each day we trust to see
The beauty of the Trinity

Love and Care for you and me
Justice, Peace, Equality,
These are the gifts God longs to see
Expressed within humanity.

But, all around, indignity;
Pride of self, and treachery
Using of others, and painfully
Our neighbour turns to enemy.

Christ, in your risen power today,
Come and transform our moral grey.
Set us on fire, in work and play
To sing the song of Trinity.

Mother, forgive them

Those that sexually harass the weak

Mother forgive them
For they know not what they do

Those that spit on my body

Mother forgive them
For they know not what they do

Those that condemn me for loose living

Mother forgive them
For they know not what they do

Those that judge me with pious words

Mother forgive them
For they know not what they do

Those that delay in treating me

Mother forgive them
For they know not what they do

Those that exploit my illness for profit and gain

Mother forgive them
For they know not what they do

Those that prevaricate and analyse endlessly

Mother forgive them
For they know not what they do

Those that fight for power, but not for those who suffer

Mother forgive them
For they know not what they do

Those that speak in hushed tones and whispers

Mother forgive them
For they know not what they do

Those that erect barbed wire around us

Mother forgive them
For they know not what they do

Remembrance litany

Sit in a circle around a table upon which are seven unlit candles. Arrange for seven people each to light a candle, and say one of the following sentences. Keep a silence after each candle is lit.

First candle
I light this candle so that we may remember all those African women sold to be slaves in the sugar plantations.

Second candle
I light this candle so that we may remember all those women slaves beaten or raped by their masters, or ill treated by their mistresses.

Third candle
I light this candle so that we may remember Hannah More and Ann Yearsley who campaigned, without tiring, against slavery.

Fourth candle
I light this candle so that we may remember Lucy Townsend, Mary Lloyd, Sarah Wedgwood, Sophia Sturge, Jane Smeal, Elizabeth Pease and Anne Knight who founded and organized women's anti-slavery societies.

Fifth candle
I light this candle so that we may remember Gemma Adams, Annelli Alderton, Annette Nicholls, Paula Clennell and Tania Nicol, the five young women who were killed in Ipswich recently.

Sixth candle
I light this candle as we pray for all the women, men and children today who are used for sex.

Seventh candle
I light this candle as we pray for all those who struggle and work today against sex-trafficking, especially ...... *(Give space for people to add their own intercessions.)*

All say:

God our Creator, Redeemer and Sustainer,
be present today with all those people who suffer this slavery today
and all those who try to support them.

Stir our hearts that we may not sit lightly to this struggle
but give ourselves to this task.
Amen.

Prayer for respect: the CHASTE Collect

Beloved God, lover of all humanity,
you called us to live together in honesty,
dignity and freedom.
We pray that in our relationships,
with our bodies, and with the bodies of others,
we remember that we were bought by your blood.

Provoke us, by the power of your Justice,
to liberate all who are trafficked today
so that your kingdom may arise
and chains be broken.
In the name of God, our Creator, Redeemer and Sustainer.
Amen.

---

www.CHASTE.org.uk

What is CHASTE?

CHASTE stands for: Churches Alert To Sex Trafficking across Europe. It is an ecumenical UK charity, working within a Christian Church context, to bring about nationwie "zero tolerance" of sex trafficking in Britain today.

What is Sex Trafficking?

Sex trafficking involves the recruitment and transportation of people, (usually women - not always), by means of threat, violence, blackmail, deception or abuse. It is rape, deceit, and naked abuse of power for the production of wealth and the provision of "leisure sex". It is highly organised, criminal and global.

CHASTE works for

Safety for victims of sex trafficking: provision of counselling, pastoral support and safe-housing. This helps enable holistic recovery and rehabilitation. CHASTE initiated the Round Table on Safe Housing provided by Christian communities in 2004.

Co-operation across churches worldwide, particularly in Africa and Eastern Europe, to respond to the pastoral needs of victims of trafficking and to provide prophetic protest and cultural leadership in a world where children, young women and men are trafficked across borders for commercialised sex

Awareness of the connections between prostitution, sex trafficking and the degradation of women and men's bodies, violence and inequality.

Awareness of the social issues revolving around "client-demand" and the impact it has on the growing "supply" of women being shipped into Britain for that "market".

To work with all NGOs and Government agencies worldwide to counter trafficking through effective legislation, culture-change and institutional capacity building.

CHASTE connections

We work with a large network of groups which include:
Baptist Mission Society Worldwide
The Conference of Religious
Campaign for the Removal of Pimps (CROP)
Churches Together in Britain and Ireland (CTBI)
Churches Together in England (CTE)
CHASTE Albania
Churches Commission on Migration in Europe
The Churches Against Trafficking network in Europe
National Christian Alliance on Prostitution (NCAP)
Edo State African Women's Co-operative
African Family Federation
Hundreds of individual Church Companions across the UK

CHASTE sits on the Board of the United Kingdom Human Trafficking Centre and works closely with the police and other agencies combating trafficking.

CHASTE Achievements

Since CHASTE's inception we have:

- worked with over 80 referred women, minors and young men who have been trafficked into the UK for sexual exploitation
- initiated a Safe Housing Round Table to develop accommodation for safety for women who have been ensnared into trafficked exploitation as a result of which three safe houses have been opened, paid for by religious denominations.
- trained chaplains and case-workers in immigration removal centres
- advised police and immigration personnel in issues centring around trafficking, based on our case-work experience
- raised awareness of the issue of trafficking in the major denominations
- initiated theological reflection on issues of gender and on the international power imbalances which are catalysts for migration, exploitation and prostitution
- facilitated work with the police and other Government departments on an ongoing project to assist trafficked women
- run the Westminster CHASTE Conference 2006 facilitating over one hundred key church representatives to respond to the UK Government consultation on proposal for a UK action plan tackling Human Trafficking
- given advice, at strategic level, to the police
- developed an IPOD reassurance package for those who are interviewed by police during raids at brothels, massage parlours and off-street locations of sexual exploitation
- run two successful postcard campaigns: "Not for sale" resulting in the ratification of the Palermo Protocol in 2006; "Time for a®rest" campaign resulting in the signing of the Council of Europe Convention in 2007
- instigated "Not For Sale Sunday", annually, on the third Sunday in May, to enable the churches in the UK to focus on this modern-day slavery – and to become activists against this terrible abuse in the UK.
- Launched Not For Sale UK to address issues of demand.

Please do contact us if you can help us realise the changes envisioned in the pages of this book. Or with queries, encouragement or a donation to our work – all our work to date has been independent of any Government funding, and it is important to open the bank vaults of heaven for this work of cultural change and immediate pastoral assistance.

contact@chaste.org.uk
Tel: 0845 456 9335
Or see our web pages for more information:
www.chaste.org.uk
www.notforsalesunday.org

BMS World Mission is a leading Christian mission organisation supporting over 320 workers based in more than 40 countries, helping the poorest of the poor in some of the world's neediest places. For more details visit www.bmsworldmission.org

CROP (Coalition for the Removal of Pimping) was founded in 1996 by Irene Ivison whose 17 year old daughter Fiona was coerced into prostitution by a pimp and then murdered by a punter. CROP supports parents of children and young people who are similarly targeted and groomed, and seeks to use their expertise to highlight the hidden violent exploitation that whole families suffer.
For more details visit www.crop1.org.uk, email crop1@freeuk.com or telephone 0113 240 3040/60

MACSAS (Minister & Clergy Sexual Abuse Survivors) is an interdenominational self help organisation supporting women and men sexually abused or exploited, as children or as adults, by clergy, ministers or religious. For our helpline call 0808 8010 340 (open on Sat: 10am-2pm, Mon: 6-10pm, Tues: 1pm-5pm) or visit us at www.macsas.org, email macsas1@hotmail.com. To subscribe to our magazine (3 times/year) write to MACSAS, PO Box 46933, London E8 1XA.

The Medaille Trust is a charity founded by Catholic nuns, brothers and priests with the aim of helping women, young men and children who have been freed from sex-trafficking. We provide safe housing and offer opportunities for physical and psychological healing and rehabilitation, are part of the CHASTE roundtable network on safe housing provision, alongside campaigning and raising awareness in the UK about the sex-trafficking industry.